Jihadi Discourse in the Wake of the Arab Spring

EXECUTIVE SUMMARY

This report analyzes jihadi discourse in the wake of the "Arab Spring" in order to address two related questions: (1) why have global jihadi leaders been struggling to advance a coherent and effective response to the events of the Arab Spring, and (2) why, despite strong rhetoric of militancy, have we witnessed little action on the part of new jihadi groups that have emerged in countries that underwent regime change (i.e., Tunisia, Egypt and Libya) as a result of the Arab Spring? To answer these questions, this study focuses on original Arabic sources in the form of public statements released by global jihadi leaders in response to the Arab Spring and by new groups projecting a jihadi worldview that have emerged in Tunisia, Egypt and Libya. Regional jihadi groups that were established prior to the Arab Spring are not the focus of this study. This study reveals that global jihadi leaders are struggling to define clearly and consistently their ideological framework in the aftermath of the Arab Spring. More precisely, the factors that are causing the current ideological incoherence of jihadism are the same factors that had once served as the cornerstone of its plausibility in the eyes of its adherents.

Global Jihadi Leaders' Discourse

This study identifies several weaknesses in the discourse of global jihadi leaders that highlight the nature of the challenges they face in the wake of the Arab Spring. These include the paradoxical position of *the deed of spectating*: the jihadis have always prided themselves on action, i.e., on the deed of jihad; and in so doing, they gained the attention of the world community. Yet, in the initial phase of the Arab Spring, the jihadis found themselves not as actors in, but as spectators of the drama of fallen dictators. Another related challenge is the once powerful grievance narrative that "jihad is the only solution" to rid Muslims of their dictators that jihadi leaders and ideologues had propagated. This narrative, however, is shaken in the wake of the Arab Spring as non-violent protest toppled some iconic dictators like Husni Mubarak of Egypt and Zein al-'Abidin bin 'Ali of Tunisia. The most glaring weakness of current jihadi discourse has to do with the fact that after the fall of dictators, people have chosen a political path that is irreconcilable with the jihadi worldview and have become the object of jihadi resentment. Thus the jihadis' once-powerful grievances articulated against dictators are now reduced to soliloquies criticizing the people.

New Jihadi Groups

In analyzing the effects of the Arab Spring on the nascent groups that have emerged in Tunisia, Egypt and Libya, it is important to distinguish between violence ensuing from the types of unrest that are typical of states undergoing regime change and that resulting from new groups projecting a jihadi agenda. These new groups uphold the principle of the obligation of jihad, advance anti-democratic rhetoric using religious arguments and lionize global jihadi leaders and their causes.

Yet, for now, new jihadi groups are characterized more by the *propaganda* of jihad than by its *delivery*. Despite their opposition not just to the regimes but to the very nature of what constitutes legitimacy, and despite their threatening militant rhetoric, they have largely refrained from translating their jihadism into action. Many among the public faces of new jihadi groups had established their credentials when they took up jihad against the *ancien régime* of dictators and as a result suffered exile or imprisonment; now they owe their new public existence to the transitioning regimes, the very regimes whose legitimacy they do not recognize. In some ways, they are like the bastard offspring of autocratic regimes and democratizing ones. While these groups have not thus far delivered the militant action their rhetoric of jihad promises, it is possible that violence may be unleashed not by the design of the leaders of these new groups, but through the actions of frustrated members (or former members), or those inspired by their militant rhetoric.

Syria

While Syria has not undergone a regime change, the proliferation of militant groups there, some of which fight under a jihadi banner, necessitates discussing it in the context of jihadi relevance in the wake of the Arab Spring. Thus, the concluding chapter of the report tackles the following question: does the violent conflict in Syria restore credibility in the jihadis' motto that "jihad is the only solution"? More precisely, does Syria give back to the jihadi narrative what Tunisia, Egypt and to some extent Libya had taken away? The concluding section argues that the events in Syria could have restored the credibility of jihadism, but competition between the Islamic State of Iraq (and the Levant) and the Syria-based jihadi group Jabhat al-Nusra (JN) has confused their supporters and earned the derision of their opponents. The divide between the two groups even risks undermining the symbolic position that Ayman al-Zawahiri occupies as the global leader of jihad.

Implications

Notwithstanding the current ideological inconsistencies that are challenging jihadi discourse and the divides that plague jihadism from within, jihadism continues to be a dangerous global phenomenon. Nevertheless, these challenges are consequential to the evolution of jihadism, its effectiveness and endurance. In the long term, when the rationale of radical violent groups begins to falter, their capacity to recruit people into the fold would suffer, as would their longevity. But in the short term the ideological incoherence and inconsistency between rhetoric and practice may cause splintering within a given group, paving the way for more radicalized factions to emerge and seek to prove their credentials through erratic violent behavior.

INTRODUCTION

The fall of dictators brought about by the initial wave of the "Arab Spring" is an aspiration many Arabs dreamed about, prayed for or attempted to pursue through political channels – an exercise that for decades seemed futile. The jihadis did not settle for dreaming or praying – although there is no shortage of either in the jihadi cultural universe. Convinced by the futility of peaceful reforms, they set out on the path of jihad intent on bringing down dictators and fighting against the Western countries that they believed supported these dictators.[1] For decades jihadis – despite their differences – have been in agreement that *jihad is the only solution* to rid Muslims of their dictators to pave the way for establishing a just society in which God's Law reigns supreme. In the words of Ayman al-Zawahiri, who has been declared by jihadi websites to be Usama Bin Ladin's successor, "there is no solution except through jihad, all other solutions are futile. Rather, other solutions would only worsen the state of dilapidation and submissiveness in which we live; [purported solutions that exclude jihad] are equivalent to treating cancer with aspirin."[2] In doing so, unlike Islamist groups that are also driven by Islamic religious teachings of social justice but chose the electoral path to advance their agenda, jihadis have rejected the world order of nation-states and the

---

[1] For the purpose of this report, unless otherwise stated, the term "jihad" is used to designate a military struggle. The other meaning of jihad designates the struggle of the individual to fulfill faithfully the religious obligations of Islam, such as daily prayer and fasting, and more generally the spiritual struggle against the temptations of worldly pleasures to improve the inner self before God in this world and on the Day of Judgment. It should be noted that jihadis draw on the classical legal doctrine of jihad and believe themselves to be carrying out defensive jihad (*jihad al-dafʻ*) as opposed to offensive jihad (*jihad al-talab*). According to the classical doctrine, whereas offensive jihad could only be launched at the authority of a legitimate ruler and stipulates several conditions as to who qualifies to carry out such a jihad, defensive jihad is an individual obligation that needn't be authorized by any superior authority and is to be carried out when the territory of Islam is invaded. For an excellent exposition of the theory of jihad, see Paul L. Heck, 'Jihad Revisited', *Journal of Religious Ethics*, 32.1: 95-128; See also Michael Bonner, *Jihad in Islamic* History, Princeton: Princeton University Press, 2006; and Majid Khadduri, 'Introduction', *The Islamic Law of Nations: Shaybānī's Siyar*, Baltimore: The Johns Hopkins Press, 1966.
[2] Ayman al-Zawahiri, "Haqa'iq al-Siraʻ bayna al-Islam wa-al-Kufr," *CTC Library*. Unless otherwise stated, translation of Arabic passages are by Nelly Lahoud.

state's monopoly on the legitimate use of physical force. Instead, jihadis have embraced jihad as the primary means of political change.[3]

But if peaceful protests could bring down Presidents Zayn al-Din bin 'Ali of Tunisia (January 2011) and Husni Mubarak of Egypt (February 2011) in the seismic phenomenon known as the "Arab Spring," where does this leave jihadism? In view of the unpredictable nature of the events that have characterized the onset and subsequent developments of the Arab Spring, a serious attempt to anticipate its future in general, and its impact on jihadism in particular, is fraught with risks. This report therefore avoids addressing ambitious questions, such as whether the Arab Spring is a success or a failure and whether it will lead to the demise of jihadism.

Instead, this report analyzes jihadi discourse since the onset of the Arab Spring in order to address two related questions: (1) why have global jihadi leaders been struggling to advance a coherent and effective response to the events of the Arab Spring, and (2) why, despite strong rhetoric of militancy, have we witnessed little action on the part of new jihadi groups that have emerged in countries that underwent regime change as a result of the Arab Spring?

The pertinence of these questions lies in the consequential effects of both the Arab Spring and jihadism on the Middle East and North Africa (MENA) region. Some analysts expressed concern that the instability brought about by the Arab Spring is engendering a fertile ground for jihadis to operate in the region. Among others, Bruce Hoffman worries that it "may create new opportunities for al-Qa`ida and its allies to regroup and reorganize,"[4] and even this instability "endowed" al-Qa'ida "with new relevance."[5] In a similar vein, others have remarked that there is a causal link between

---

[3] On the ideological distinctions that separate Islamists from jihadis, see Nelly Lahoud, "The Strengths and Weaknesses of Jihadist Ideology," *CTC Sentinel*, 1 October 2010.
[4] Bruce Hoffman, "The Arab Spring and its Influence on al-Qa'ida," *CTC Sentinel*, 22 May 2012.
[5] Bruce Hoffman, "Al Qaeda's Uncertain Future," *Studies in Conflict and Terrorism*, 36: 635-653, 2013, p. 636.

the Arab Spring and the rise of new jihadi groups, warning that this may lead to a violent conflict that would destabilize the newly elected regimes.[6] Such concerns invariably point to cohesion on both the ideological and operational levels that jihadism is said to enjoy, suggesting the possibility that the Arab Spring serves not only to strengthen, but also to enhance its violent output.

This study argues that the complex dynamics introduced by the Arab Spring have not all been favorable to jihadis: through a close reading of their Arabic public statements, this study reveals that global jihadi leaders are struggling to define clearly and consistently their ideological framework in the aftermath of the Arab Spring, and that new jihadi groups that have emerged in Tunisia, Egypt and Libya are not delivering the militant action their rhetoric of jihad promises. The arguments this study advances require qualifications. It should be acknowledged that jihadi leaders are not alone in struggling to provide an effective response to the Arab Spring; indeed, the international community as a whole is struggling in its response to the Arab Spring. Further, every group or movement is bound to suffer from a degree of ideological incoherence, and jihadism should not be held to an impossible standard. However, as will be explained below, the factors that are causing the current ideological incoherence of jihadism are the same factors that had once served as the cornerstone of its plausibility in the eyes of its adherents. As to nascent jihadi groups that have emerged in the wake of the Arab Spring, while it is still premature to provide a solid assessment of these groups, the current gap between their rhetoric and their deeds is nevertheless significant enough to warrant questioning of their overall claims and effectiveness as *bona fide* jihadi groups.

---

[6] Among others, Peter Beaumont and Patrick Kingsley, "Violent tide of Salafism threatens the Arab Spring," *The Guardian*, 9 February 2013, http://www.guardian.co.uk/world/2013/feb/09/violent-salafists-threaten-arab-spring-democracies (accessed 28 May 2013); Robert F. Worth, "Jihadists' Surge in North Africa Reveals Grim Side of Arab Spring," *The New York Times*, 19 January 2013, http://www.nytimes.com/2013/01/20/world/africa/in-chaos-in-north-africa-a-grim-side-of-arab-spring.html?pagewanted=all&_r=0 (accessed 28 May 2013); Daveed Gartenstein-Ross and Tara Vassefi, "Perceptions of the "Arab Spring" within the Salafi-Jihadi Movement," *Studies in Conflict and Terrorism*, 35:831-848, 2012.

The current inconsistencies of jihadism are consequential to its evolution, effectiveness and endurance as a global phenomenon. Violent radical groups define themselves by rationales that sustain their worldview, give meaning to their actions,[7] and ultimately determine their longevity.[8] When the rationale of such a group begins to falter, it stands to reason that in the long term its capacity to recruit people into the fold would suffer, as would its longevity. But in the short term the ideological internal incoherence and inconsistency between rhetoric and practice may cause splintering within the group, paving the way for more radicalized factions to emerge that seek to prove their credentials through erratic violent behavior.[9]

Parameters of the Study

Global Jihadi Discourse

To analyze the changes in jihadi discourse, this study focuses on public statements released by global jihadi leaders in response to the Arab Spring (Chapter One). If one is to define leadership according to jihadi parlance, every jihadi is a leader and every jihadi is meant to be carrying a global mission, since jihadism does not acknowledge the legitimacy of borders that define nation-states. But for the purpose of this study, the category of global jihadi leaders is limited to those who are perceived by jihadis – and by those of us who study them – to be speaking to a global audience; they are also perceived to influence and earn, in public, the respect of the leaders of regional jihadi groups such as Harakat al-Shabab al-Mujahidin, in Somalia, and al-Qa'ida in the Arabian Peninsula (AQAP), in Yemen. While declassified captured battlefield documents reveal that the influence of global jihadi leaders on regional jihadi groups is

---

[7] Martha Crenshaw, "The Causes of Terrorism," *Comparative Politics*, Vol. 13, No. 4, July 1981.

[8] David C. Rapoport, 'The Four Waves of Modern Terrorism', in Audrey Kurth Cronin and James M. Ludes (eds), Attacking Terrorism: Elements of a Grand Strategy, Washington, D.C.: Georgetown University Press, 2004, pp. 46-73.

[9] Audrey Kurth Cronin, 'How al-Qaida Ends: the Decline and Demise of Terrorist Groups,' *International Security*, Vol. 31, No. 1 (Summer 2006), pp. 7-48. See also Nelly Lahoud, *The Jihadi's Path to Self-Destruction*, New York/London: Columbia University Press/Hurst, 2010, "Chapter Five."

more symbolic than real,[10] it is the existence of global jihadi leaders that conveys a

perception of a global jihadi community, however imagined this community may be.

For example, the symbolic global leadership of figures such as Bin Ladin (d. May 2011)

and al-Zawahiri is uncontested.[11] Others such as 'Atiyyatullah/'Atiyya al-Libi (d.

August 2011) and Abu Yahya al-Libi (d. June 2012) can also be grouped under the

umbrella of global jihadi leaders. In addition to being recognizable public faces of

jihadism, the released documents from Bin Ladin's Abbottabad compound show that in

his last year, Bin Ladin had a close working relationship with 'Atiyya,[12] and that he also

held respect for Abu Yahya's literary abilities.[13] In jihadi circles, these leaders are

considered to be "shuyukh al-jihad" (Sheikhs of jihad), a statusthat recognizes their

sacrifices and precedence in jihad. Their leadership is not limited to a region: they are

leaders in Tanzim al-Qa'ida (the organization of al-Qa'ida), a global organization since

its inception,[14] and in more recent years, in Qa'idat al-Jihad (The Base of Jihad), a name

that al-Zawahiri has progressively used.[15] It is for this reason that their public

statements in response to the Arab Spring are analyzed in this study.

---

[10] See Nelly Lahoud, Stuart Caudill, Liam Collins, Gabriel Koehler-Derrick, Muhammad al-'Ubaydi and Don Rassler, "Letters from Abbottabad: Bin Ladin Sidelined?," *CTC Report*, 3 May 2012.

[11] For an informative account of Bin Ladin's life, see Jonathan Randal, *Osama: The Making of a Terrorist*, Vintage, 2005; an authoritative account of al-Zawahiri's life is yet to be written, but it is worth consulting Muntasir al-Zayyat, *al-Zawahiri kama 'Araftuhu*, Cairo: Dar Misr al-Mahrusa, 2nd edition, 2002.

[12] For more on his jihadi career, see Ayman al-Zawahiri's eulogy of 'Atiyya, "Risalat al-amal wa al-bishr li ahlina fi Misr" (8), CTC Library. His real name is Jamal Ibrahim Ishtiwi al-Misrati and is also known by two aliases, namely Abu `Abd al-Rahman and `Atiyyatullah, 'Atiyya is short for the latter. He was born in 1970 in Misrata, Libya, pursued Islamic religious studies in Mauritania, then joined jihad in Algeria. He went to Afghanistan in the late 1990s and was killed in a drone strike in Pakistan on 22 August 2011.

[13] Usama b. Ladin, SOCOM-2012-0000010. See also Michael Moss and Souad Mekhennet, "Rising Leader for Next Phase of Al Qaeda's War," *The New York Times*, April 4, 2008, http://www.nytimes.com/2008/04/04/world/asia/04qaeda.html?pagewanted=all&_r=0 (accessed 4 August 2013). His real name is Hasan Qa'id and a former member of the Libyan Islamic Fighting Group. He traveled to Afghanistan in the early 1990s, then pursued Islamic religious studies in Mauritania before returning to Afghanistan. He was captured a year after 9/11 by Pakistani authorities and handed to U.S. authorities where he was imprisoned in Bagram prison. He and several other jihadis escaped on 10 July 2005.

[14] On al-Qa'ida's global dimension and uniqueness in the jihadi landscape, see Nelly Lahoud, "Beware of Imitators: al-Qa'ida through the Lens of its Confidential Secretary," *CTC Report*, 4 June 2012, particularly pp. 37-41.

[15] Nelly Lahoud has alluded to a certain mystery, possibly internal differences between al-Zawahiri and Bin Ladin, who never used the name "Qa'idat al-Jihad" in his public statements. See footnote 6 in her "The Merger of al-Shabab and Qa'idat al-Jihad," *CTC Sentinel*, 16 February 2012.

In addition, the American-born Adam Gadahn is arguably another global jihadi leader who clearly enjoyed the trust and respect of Bin Ladin.[16] Even though it is not clear whether he enjoys the same global appeal as the others,[17] his public statements address the global umma and he has also released his own reflections about the Arab Spring, which will be analyzed in this study. In recent months, a certain Husam 'Abd al-Ra'uf has surfaced in jihadi media: 'Abd al-Ra'uf has been part of the jihadi scene since 1989, but it is only in June 2013 that he released his first audio public statement, "Risala li-al-Umma" (Missive to the Umma), that touched on the events of the Arab Spring. It is possible that he is being promoted as a candidate who might succeed al-Zawahiri. Since his statement was produced by al-Sahab and published by al-Fajr, the two media outlets of al-Qa'ida, we are therefore invited to assume that he too may qualify as a global jihadi leader.

However, the statements of regional jihadi groups are not analyzed in this study. While leaders of these groups claim to be serving the interests of the global umma, they do not claim or project themselves to speak on behalf of those outside their territorial sphere of influence. This is evident even from their names, which are all associated with specific regions, e.g., al-Qa'ida in the Islamic *Maghreb*, al-Shabab in *Somalia*, and the Islamic State of *Iraq and the Levant*. Also omitted from this study are the statements by online pundits. Although they occupy an important space in the universe of jihadism online, and therefore contribute to the perception of a global jihadi community, the standing of these pundits in the eyes of their readers is highly volatile. For example, recognizable pundits such as Asad al-Jihad 2 and 'Abdallah bin Muhammad have in recent months (in the latter part of 2013) lost their credibility in the eyes of many readers when they criticized the Islamic State of Iraq, especially after its attempt to merge with the Syrian-

---

[16] Brian Dodwell, "The Abbottabad Documents: The Quiet Ascent of Adam Gadahn," *CTC Sentinel*, 22 May 2012.
[17] Concerning the doubts as to Gadahn's broad appeal, see the article that discusses his letter that was found in Bin Ladin's compound in Abbottabad, "Watha'iq Abbottabad al-Muqaddasa," *Shabakat al-Shumukh al-Islamiyya*, 24 October 2013, https://shamikh1.info/vb/showthread.php?t=213042 (accessed on the same day).

based jihadi group Jabhat al-Nusra.[18] It is also the case that jihadi websites are experiencing a shortage of articles authored by pundits who regularly contributed to these websites.[19] For these reasons and more, it is difficult to present a systematic study of jihadi pundits' writings.

New Jihadi Groups

To analyze the effects of the Arab Spring on countries that underwent regime change since its onset, this study focuses on new groups that have emerged in Tunisia, Egypt and Libya and are projecting a jihadi agenda (Chapter Two). While Yemen and Syria have also been affected by the Arab Spring, Yemen cannot be said to have undergone a regime change like the other three countries. The transfer of power from President 'Abdallah Saleh to his Vice President 'Abd Rabbuh Mansour Hadi, who was declared President in February 2012 after an election in which he was the only candidate, represents a cosmetic change. Despite the significant impact of the Arab Spring on Syria, at the time of writing this report it has not undergone a regime change.[20] However, because the war in Syria has attracted jihadis from different parts of the world to the fight, its effects on jihadism will be discussed in the concluding chapter of this report.

In analyzing the effects of the Arab Spring on jihadism in Tunisia, Egypt and Libya, it is important to distinguish between violence ensuing from the types of unrest that are typical of states undergoing regime change and that resulting from new groups projecting a jihadi agenda. Scholars have long observed that states undergoing sudden

---

[18] See for example the article criticizing 'Abdallah bin Muhammad, entitled "Kashf ma Alqahu Iblis min al-Bahraj wa-al-Talbis 'ala Qalb 'Abdallah bin Muhammad al-Ta'is," *Shabakat Shumukh al-Islam*, 15 April 2013, https://shamikh1.info/vb/showthread.php?t=198388 (accessed 18 April 2013).

[19] See for example the article by Mu'awiya al-Qahtani in which he laments this shortage: "Ilyakum al-Su'al al-Mu'lim ya Al al-Shumukh," *Shabakat Shumukh al-Islam*, http://www.shamikh1.info/vb/showthread.php?t=184647 (accessed 9 November 2012). The scarcity of contributions by pundits is noticeable, including general quietude on the part of Abu Hafs al-Sunni al-Sunni, Abu Fadl al-Madi, and Husayn bin Mahamud.

[20] This report was completed on 25 October 2013.

regime change, particularly those transitioning from an autocratic regime and attempting to forge a democratic path, are likely to experience instability, civil violence, and even war.[21] There are indeed some trends to this effect in countries that underwent regime change since the onset of the Arab Spring. For example, Tunisia continues to suffer from intermittent unrest: in February 2013 the assassination of the politician Chukri Belaid, known for his secular views, sparked protests that led to the resignation of the Prime Minister Hamadi Jabali; the unrest was heightened six months later when another politician, Mohamed Brahmi – leader of the opposition party Movement of the People – was assassinated.[22]

Egypt's unrest is of an even higher magnitude: its 25 January 2011 revolution has been supplanted by mass protests calling for the resignation of the elected President, Muhammad Mursi, and his government. Days later the Egyptian military forcibly ousted the President, detained him and appointed an interim government headed by a judge.[23] The power struggle between Mursi's supporters and the military has resulted in the deaths of hundreds of protestors.[24]

Libya's weak central authority has made it even more vulnerable to intermittent violence, particularly as militias continue to comprise a significant part of the security apparatus of the country. The killing of the U.S. Ambassador to Libya Chris Stevens in September 2012 and of 'Abdul-Salam al-Musmari, who is reported to be a "prominent

---

[21] See for example the classical studies by Edward D. Mansfield and Jack Snyder, "Democratization and the Danger of War," *International Security*, Vol. 20, Issue 1, Summer 1995, pp. 5-38; *Electing to Fight: Why Emerging Democracies Go to War*, Cambridge: The MIT Press, 2007, see chapters 1 and 3.

[22] "Tunisian politician Mohamed Brahmi assassinated," *BBC*, 25 July 2013, http://www.bbc.co.uk/news/world-africa-23452979, (accessed 31 July 2013).

[23] David D. Kirkpatrick, "Army Ousts Egypt's President; Mursi is Taken into Military Custody," *The New York Times*, 3 July 2013, http://www.nytimes.com/2013/07/04/world/middleeast/egypt.html?pagewanted=all&_r=0 (accessed 31 July 2013).

[24] "Violence in Egypt: Digging in ever Deeper," *The Economist*, 29 July 2013, http://www.economist.com/blogs/pomegranate/2013/07/violence-egypt (accessed 31 July 2013). At the time of this study (end of October 2013), the struggle between the military and Mursi's supporters is ongoing. See "Ansar Mursi Yad'una li-al-Tazahur fi Midan al-Tahrir al-Jum'a wa-Irtifa' Qatla Ishtibakat al-Ahad ila 53," *BBC*, 7 October 2013, http://www.bbc.co.uk/arabic/middleeast/2013/10/131006_egypt_new_callforrally_deathtoll.shtml (accessed on the same day).

critic" of the Muslim Brotherhood, in July 2013 have been followed by waves of violent unrest that have shaken the government.[25] Notwithstanding this turbulent unrest, for the most part such violence is generated independent of jihadism.[26]

The Arab Spring: Jihadi Discourse and New Jihadi Groups

From a jihadi perspective, the world is simple to describe and, more importantly, easy to criticize when dictators reign with no active opposition by the majority of the people they govern, and are supported by Western democracies.[27] That is because the jihadis' articulate criticisms of political injustices have been difficult to refute. As a result, their narrative has resonated with many in the Arab world, including those who have not joined them or do not share their agenda. The events of the Arab Spring have shaken the simplicity of the jihadi narrative now that it has been proven that dictators can be ousted by peaceful protest. To be fair, despite being surprised along with the rest of the international community by the sudden onset of the Arab Spring, global jihadi leaders initially responded with a sense of genuine optimism. In public and private communications, Bin Ladin declared the Arab Spring to be a "great historical event,"[28] and 'Atiyyatullah al-Libi, or 'Atiyya, as he is widely known, welcomed it with "enthusiasm and ardor."[29] However, Bin Ladin and 'Atiyya did not live long enough to witness the people of Tunisia, Egypt and Libya rush to cast their votes in their respective elections. In doing so, they clearly demonstrated their desire to pursue political reform by means of electoral change, a path irreconcilable with the jihadi worldview. Indeed, the formation of political parties, contesting elections and the

---

[25] "Islamist Party Office Attacked as Libya Violence Persists," *Reuters*, 29 July 2013, http://www.reuters.com/article/2013/07/29/us-libya-benghazi-idUSBRE96S0XT20130729 (accessed 31 July 2013).

[26] With respect to the jihadi violence in Sinai, in Egypt, see Chapter Two of this study.

[27] The lack of Western democracies' support for countries such as Syria was not due to its dictatorship but rather to its alliance with Iran.

[28] Usama b. Ladin, "Kalimat Shahid al-Islam – Kama Nahsabuhu – li-Ummatihi al-Muslima," released by al-Sahab, May 19, 2011, CTC Library.

[29] 'Atiyyatullah Abi 'Abd al-Rahman, "Thawrat al-Shu'ub wa-Suqut al-Nizam al-'Arabi al-Fasid," 16 February 2011, CTC Library.

establishment of democratic regimes are all rejected by jihadis; they deem such processes to be guided by positive law (i.e., man-made law) and, and in their minds, holding elections constitute a violation of God's Law.[30] That is because jihadis not only wish to project a puritanical application of God's Law, but also because they want Islamic Law to serve as an alternative governance paradigm to that of the world order of nation-states against which they rebel. This alternative religious paradigm also allows them to focus their agenda on repelling external occupiers and fighting against Muslim leaders whom they consider to be advancing a Western agenda against the interests of Muslims.

However, Abu Yahya al-Libi – who lived until June 2012 – and Ayman al-Zawahiri, Adam Gadahn and Husam 'Abd al-Ra'uf – who are still alive and releasing statements in response to the Arab Spring – saw for themselves that the political transformation of countries that underwent regime change did not follow a path that would remotely accommodate the jihadi agenda. In October 2011, almost 52 percent of Tunisians turned out to vote in the legislative elections; in January and February 2012, almost 52 percent of Egyptians voted in the legislative elections; and in July 2012, almost 62 percent of Libyans chose to vote in their legislative elections.[31] When jihadi leaders' calls to shun positive law and embrace God's Law to "protect the fruits of the revolutions" went heedless, a sense of jihadi despair set in. This translated into confusion in the discourse of global jihadi leaders who gradually began to introduce a series of qualifications and caveats, warning that unless carefully exploited, the revolutions could be reduced to a Western ploy to entrap Muslims in democracy's "more spacious" prison, in Abu Yahya's parlance.

---

[30] Jihadi writings are littered with rejections of elections and democracy. See for example Ayman al-Zawahiri, *al-Hisad al-Murr: al-Ikhwan al-Muslimun fi Sittina 'Aman, Minbar al-Tawhid wa-al-Jihad*, http://www.tawhed.ws/r?i=2gxseb4t (accessed 2 August 2013), see in particular the chapter titled "Mawqif al-Ikhwan min al-Intikhabat wa-al-barlaman."

[31] See *Election Guide*, http://www.electionguide.org/

But the ideological dilemma for jihadis goes farther than simply a fluctuation between optimism and despair. The key weakness they are facing lies with the fact that their current grievances are not with the dictator, but with the people who are choosing the ballot box. The events of the Arab Spring have shown that once freed from the yoke of dictatorship, people do not consider that the electoral path undermines their commitment to the Islamic faith. This was most evident with political parties running on Islamist and Salafi platforms, but even political parties committed to secular and liberal views did not run on anti-religious platforms. The jihadis, however, had hoped that the removal of dictators would lead to people forging an Islamic path divorced from the international world order of nation-states. Anything short of such a path, the jihadis assert, would give legitimacy to positive law and it would in turn violate God's Law. The jihadis therefore have to confront the reality that their worldview is irreconcilable with the people's choices.

What is emerging in the statements of global jihadi leaders – implicitly and at times explicitly – is a discourse focusing on the political shortcomings of the people. In this regard some jihadi leaders are more diplomatic and sensitive in articulating their concerns than others. Bin Ladin, for instance, speaks of the need "to counsel" or "to advise" the people so that they may come to realize that they are better off with establishing an Islamic state divorced from the international community. Abu Yahya is less charitable: his description of the people swapping dictatorship for a "spacious prison" implies that people are not alert to what seems to him to be common sense. Most patronizing is 'Abd al-Ra'uf, whose first – and so far only – audio statement addressed to the umma begins with a "rebuke" ('itab) of the people "for their silence and their preoccupation with worldly concerns," thereby abandoning Muslims who are suffering from massacres in different parts of the world. Reminiscent of leftist revolutionary discourse that tends to show contempt for the lack of political consciousness of the masses while at the same time depending on their mobilization, he goes on to state that "the people continue to be driven by their natural instinct and they merely need someone in whom they can trust so that he may guide them and lead them to their happiness in this world and the next."[32]

Al-Zawahiri's high profile means that he, more than others, shoulders the burden of providing a coherent ideological framework in these difficult and changing times. But he too is struggling to identify a framework that would reconcile the need of the people to assert their rights and the jihadis' interpretation of Islamic Law. Most challenging for him is his outright rejection of democracy and elections while at the same time acknowledging, indeed extolling people to demand their rights and rebel against their dictators. Perhaps realizing that his discourse was not resonating with the people's desire to participate in elections, in one statement he remarks that jihadis do not object to the principle that the umma should elect its leaders, claiming that it was through the "consensus of the umma" (*ijma' al-umma*) that the Rightly-Guided Caliphs were appointed.[33] The latter are the first four Caliphs who succeeded the Prophet Muhammad; the history of the era during which they reigned is for the most part a turbulent one, but mainstream Muslims generally accept that it was an ideal era of governance.[34] While Muslim legal scholars relate that these rulers were appointed through the "consensus of the umma," Muslim annalists do not hide the divisions that marred the Muslim community, particularly during the reigns of the third and fourth Caliphs.

Al-Zawahiri would likely find it difficult to provide a framework whereby people could elect their leaders without elections, and to reconcile this with Shari'a dictates. The

[32] Husam 'Abd al-Ra'uf, "Risala li-al-Umma," June 2013, CTC Library.
[33] Ayman al-Zawahiri,"Sittatun wa-Arba'un 'Aman 'ala 'Am al-Naksa," *Shabakat Shumukh al-Islam*, https://shamikh1.info/vb/showthread.php?t=208319 (accessed 2 August 2013).
[34] On the four Rightly-Guided Caliphs or the four-caliph thesis and its rapid spread in the ninth century, see Patricia Crone, *God's Rule: Government and Islam*, New York: Columbia University Press, 2004, pp. 27-8.

difficulty is mainly due to the confinement of egalitarianism in jihadi ideology to the battlefield. That is to say that while jihadi ideology calls on its adherents to exercise their own interpretation of Islam in so far as carrying out their jihad, as with any monotheist ideology its governance paradigm is based on a pre-modern vision of the world. It is a normative vision that privileges the educated elites when it comes to appointing a ruler and interpreting the dictates of religion in regulating the private and public spheres, thereby marginalizing the voice of the masses in the overall governance of a polity.

But the feeble jihadi narrative has not stopped some in Tunisia, Egypt and Libya from finding a space in which the jihadi message without its militant program can be sustained and promoted. Taking advantage of the new governments' prisoner releases and the new, if limited, freedoms brought about by the Arab Spring, new groups consisting of former jihadis and some new faithful have been publicly projecting a jihadi worldview and championing global jihadi causes.

Has the Arab Spring then offered a fertile ground for jihadis to flourish, as some analysts warn? While it is true that the public space occupied by these groups owes its existence to the newly acquired freedoms resulting from the Arab Spring, it is also the case that their reluctance to engage in violence can be attributed to the Arab Spring. As Chapter Two of this study shows, the growth in the number of such groups does not necessarily reflect the strength of traditional jihadism through active militancy. Instead, these groups appear to be more interested in the rhetoric of jihad than in acting on it.

For example, despite the political turmoil that Tunisia, Egypt and Libya have undergone since the onset of the Arab Spring, jihadism has failed to have an appreciable effect on the course of the political transition in these countries. Instead, what is projected to be a local jihadi landscape in solidarity with a global jihadi project is largely made up of vocal groups rallying behind "Ansar al-Shari'a" (partisans of

Shari'a), which serves as a motto and a name for some of these groups. They reject the legitimacy of the secular political process premised on positive law, deeming it to be a violation of their commitment to "tawhid" (passion for divine unity). In practical terms, proponents of this trend are anti-democratic and desire to transform the nature of the political establishment so that both the public and private spheres are governed by Islamic Law. The motto "Ansar al-Shari'a" is intended to highlight their commitment to Shari'a as incorruptible and to distinguish them from other fellow Muslims who, in their minds, have deviated from the true path of Shari'a by virtue of accepting the legitimacy of positive law.

Judging by the statements of the new jihadi groups, it is clear that they lack a solid and internally coherent ideological foundation. It is understandable that in view of the sudden and unexpected political transformations of Tunisia, Egypt and Libya, the political identity of these new groups should take time to develop. That is perhaps why in May of 2012, approximately a year after most of the groups had formed, Abu Mundhir al-Shanqiti wrote a short essay explaining what is – or rather what should be – meant by "Ansar al-Shari'a." Al-Shanqiti positions himself as a legal scholar and responds to questions seeking specific legal opinion; it is possible that he also wants to position himself as the ideologue of jihadism in the post-Arab Spring era. His writings are posted on *Minbar al-Tawhid wa-al-Jihad*, a website devoted to jihadi ideological materials and praised by numerous jihadi leaders and ideologues.[35]

In his expressively titled essay "Nahnu Ansar al-Shari'a" (We are the Partisans of Shari'a), al-Shanqiti explains that there can be no better and more sincere description of those who come together to establish God's religion than to call themselves "Ansar al-Shari'a." While the generality and even vagueness of the description may lend itself to a sense of inclusivity, it is instead *exclusivity*, by way of distinguishing some Muslims

---

[35] The website may be accessed on: www.tawhed.ws

from others, that al-Shanqiti is aiming to establish in his essay. More precisely, al-Shanqiti seeks to create an alternative political platform to that provided by the secular movers of the Arab Spring: "since there are those who associate their names with terms such as 'justice,' 'freedom,' 'development,' 'reform' and 'light' … we shall associate our name with al-Shari'a."[36] In doing so, al-Shanqiti is highlighting two issues that he believes need to be addressed following the Arab Spring: the first is to introduce a distinction between new jihadi groups calling themselves "Ansar al-Shari'a" (or a variation on the expression) and those who call themselves "Salafis"; the second is to educate the public (and even jihadis) that those who call themselves "Salafi-Jihadis" are not exclusively preoccupied with jihad.

Why does the designation "Salafis" worry al-Shanqiti? In its literal sense, the term "Salafis" designates those who adhere to the teachings of the early generation of Muslims, or "righteous predecessors" (*al-salaf al-salih*). But the term has acquired different connotations and its definition is subject to considerable debate by those who call themselves Salafis and those who study their ideology.[37] Up until the Arab Spring it was commonly assumed that Salafis were at least ultra-conservatives who do not believe in the legitimacy of positive law, or at most ultra-conservatives and supporters of jihad against the state. But when Salafis formed political parties and contested elections following the Arab Spring, the term, in al-Shanqiti's mind, became shrouded with dubiousness. In his words:

> The Salafis do not perform jihad
>
> The Salafis support the tyrants (*al-tawaghit*)

---

[36] Abu al-Mundhir al-Shanqiti, "Nahnu Ansar al-Shari'a," *Minbar al-Tawhid wa-al-Jihad*, 29 May 2012, http://www.tawhed.ws/a?a=shanqeet (accessed 29 May 2013).

[37] Ahmad Moussalli, "Wahhabism, Salafism, and Islamism: who is the Enemy?" *A Conflicts Forum Monograph*, 30 January 2009; Bernard Haykel, "On the Nature of Salafi Thought and Action," in Roel Meijer (ed.), *Global Salafism: Islam's New Religious Movement*, London: Hurst, 2009; For a critique of the use of the term "Salafi," see Christina Hellmich, "Creating the Ideology of Al Qaeda: From Hypocrites to Salafi Jihadists," *Studies in conflict and Terrorism*, 31, 2008, pp. 111-124.

The Salafis partake in democracy[38]

As to the designation "Salafi-Jihadis," al-Shanqiti believes that although it is more specific and a more faithful designation than "Salafis," it gives the impression that its adherents "do nothing other than jihad ... which is a major confusion." That is why, he argues, "Ansar al-Shari'a" is a more comprehensive designation and is "uncontested by anyone who is serious about applying God's religion" in the public and private affairs of society. In practical terms, he wants these new Ansars to focus their efforts not just on jihad but more importantly on forming a "public opinion" rivaling that of the secularists, one that "spreads the pure creed," "warns against democracy and positive law," and "mobilizes the Muslim Street using an Islamic legal discourse." It should be noted that al-Shanqiti's views do not represent all new jihadis. As observed earlier, his essay was published a year after many groups were formed: those who did not call themselves "Ansar al-Shari'a" remain keen to preserve their affiliation with Salafism.[39]

If al-Shanqiti is trying to enrich the ideological discourse of new jihadi groups, he does not entirely succeed. For example, it is not clear why the designation "Ansar al-Shari'a" solves the problem that, in his mind, the term "Salafis" does not. Al-Shanqiti may have forgotten that some of today's "Salafis" made the same argument about their name to distinguish their religious commitment from Muslims who form political parties and participate in elections. What would he do if a proportion of the new jihadi groups calling themselves Ansar al-Shari'a decided to form political parties and contest elections? Al-Shanqiti would have no choice but to adopt a different designation.

---

[38] Abu al-Mundhir al-Shanqiti, "Nahnu Ansar al-Shari'a," *Minbar al-Tawhid wa-al-Jihad*, 29 May 2012, http://www.tawhed.ws/a?a=shanqeet (accessed 29 May 2013).

[39] Further, his rigid opinions, particularly those against the Free Syrian Army, have earned him serious criticisms from within jihadi circles. The London-based ideologue, Abu Basir al-Tartusi, who is pushing for pragmatism in defining who is legitimate among the Syrian rebels, accused al-Shanqiti of "extremism." He also remarked that al-Shanqiti's elaborate citations of legal arguments are intended to show off his knowledge rather than provide sound legal basis for the matters he treats. See Abu Basir al-Tartusi, "Su'al 'an Abi al-Mundhir al-Shanqiti," http://tartosi.blogspot.com/2012/11/blog-post_13.html (accessed 29 May 2013).

Beyond the ideological pedestrianism resulting from their nascent emergence, the glaring difference between new jihadi groups and traditional jihadism is their commitment to action. While traditional jihadism encompasses cleavages and factions that suffer from ideological simplicity and incoherence, traditional jihadis are generally committed to the deed of jihad. However, when it comes to the role of jihad in making God's Law reign supreme, new jihadi groups seem to be content with focusing their energy on rhetoric rather than on action. For instance, traditional jihadism saw *tawhid* and jihad as two sides of the same coin: in the jihadis' parlance, *tawhid* serves as an alternative paradigm to positive law; the latter is necessarily defective on account of being the product of man-made laws, lacking the perfection of a Just Legislator. Believers who adopt *tawhid* are thus liberated from having to worship imperfect and unjust laws that serve the interests of a minority of humans and instead devote themselves to worshipping the just divine Law. To justify the merit of *tawhid*, traditional jihadi discourse highlights the injustices inflicted upon Muslims to rationalize mounting jihad against their enemies. More precisely, jihad is meant to rid Muslims of their oppressive dictators and bring about, through *tawhid*, justice in this world, and thereby earn a place in paradise. As such, traditional jihadism dismisses any solution that does not support the legitimacy of jihad to implement *tawhid*.

However, even though jihadi groups that have emerged in countries that underwent regime change are preoccupied with extolling the virtues of *tawhid*, they seem less inclined to resort to jihad to bring it about. For example, while their discourse seeks to undermine the legitimacy of positive law and the political processes that flow from it, they appear neither prepared to abandon jihad explicitly nor inclined to promote it in an active fashion. In short, whereas jihad is a vocation for traditional jihadis, for now, new jihadi groups seem to be taking a vacation from jihad.

How then are we to understand the political identity of these new groups? Can there be jihadis without jihad? While thus far jihadism has been a relatively insignificant element in the changes affecting the political visage of countries that underwent regime change in the MENA region, one cannot surmise that such a trend will persist. Indeed, the Arab Spring is an evolving political phenomenon, a work in progress, the dynamics of which will be influenced in the years to come by a range of domestic, regional and international factors.

Syria

With respect to the relevance of jihadism to the future of the region, a key factor likely to have a significant impact concerns the militant landscape in Syria. That is why an assessment of jihadism in Tunisia, Egypt and Libya should not ignore the possibility that a prolonged conflict in Syria will serve to empower jihadi elements there and elsewhere, ultimately giving increased significance to jihadism in the region. If Syria were to become "worse than Somalia" as the Joint Special Representative of the UN and the Arab League for Syria Lakhdar Brahimi fears, it stands to reason that a failed Syrian state would be a magnet for global jihadis – where there is already an influx of foreign fighters.[40] Syria's proximity to Israel is undoubtedly an appealing feature to those jihadis who have longed to "liberate al-Aqsa," by which they mean Palestine, but who were persuaded by various jihadi leaders that the march on al-Aqsa begins in Afghanistan, Iraq, or Kashmir.[41]

---

[40]See for example the announcement of "Katibat al-Muhajirin," *al-Shumukh*, 17 March 2013, https://shamikh1.info/vb/showthread.php?t=195226 (accessed 7 May 2013); Sergei Boeke and Daan Weggemans, "Destination Jihad: Why Syria and not Mali," *International Center for Counter-Terrorism – The Hague (ICCT)*, 10 April 2013, http://www.icct.nl/publications/icct-commentaries/destination-jihad-why-syria-and-not-mali?dm_i=1ADT,1G1AA,76AWSE,4WL92,1, (accessed 7 May 2013).

[41] For a classical argument, see 'Abdallah 'Azzam, *Dhikrayat Filastin, Minbar al-Tawhid wa-al-Jihad*, http://www.tawhed.ws/a?a=a82qriko (accessed 8 May 2013); See also Ayman al-Zawahiri, "al-Quds lan Tuhawwad," 20 July 2010, *CTC* Library;

In view of the effective battlefield role the jihadi group Jabhat al-Nusra (JN) is performing in Syria, even in the eyes of other Syrian opposition battlefield leaders,[42] it could potentially give momentum to jihadism. The concluding section of this study explores the fate of jihadism as it relates to Syria and asks whether the violent conflict in Syria restores faith in the ideal that "jihad is the only solution." This study concludes that while Syria has indeed broken the relatively peaceful pattern set by Tunisians, Egyptians and to a lesser extent Libyans in ousting their respective dictators, and while it has also given jihadis a bold new vocation, the jihadis' public divisions, not least the division between JN and the Islamic State of Iraq (now renamed the Islamic State in Iraq and the Levant) are beginning to discredit them. Further, Syria is providing a space for enthusiasts from Tunisia, Egypt and Libya needing to translate the rhetoric of jihad into action: paradoxically, the violent arena in Syria is sparing their home countries the security instability they might otherwise cause.

---

[42] See for example the interview with by Salim Idris, head of the Free Syrian Army's Supreme Military Council, in which he lauded their operational capacity and professionalism, 6 March 2013, http://www.youtube.com/watch?v=1yeuqyIt8WI (accessed 7 May 2013); see also the interview with Riyad al-As'ad, the leader of the Free Syrian Army, 19 March 2013, https://www.youtube.com/watch?v=RWrZhQG4leg&feature=player_embedded (accessed 7 May 2013).

The "Arab Spring": The Response of Shuyukh (Sheikhs) Al-Jihad

This chapter analyzes the public statements of global jihadi leaders in response to the series of events known as the "Arab Spring" to explore its impact on the effectiveness of their discourse. Statements analyzed are by those who many jihadis have come to consider as "shuyukh al-jihad" (Sheikhs of Jihad), namely Usama Bin Ladin, 'Atiyyatullah al-Libi, Abu Yahya al-Libi and Ayman al-Zawahiri. Also included is an analysis of the statements by Adam Gadahn and Husam 'Abd al-Ra'uf, both of whom responded to the events of the Arab Spring.[43] A close reading of the statements of these leaders shows that they are struggling to advance a coherent and effective response to the events of the Arab Spring, and this chapter addresses the reasons underpinning the challenges they face.

The chapter consists of two sections. The first section identifies the main challenges to jihadism in the aftermath of the Arab Spring, while the second presents a textual analysis of the statements of global jihadi leaders, highlighting their struggle to present a coherent ideological framework. The chapter argues that jihadism suffers from several challenges posed by the circumstances inherent in the aftermath of the Arab Spring, including: that the jihadis' role, at least initially, was that of spectators of – rather than actors in – the drama of fallen dictators; that the success of peaceful protests in bringing down the Presidents of Tunisia and Egypt undermined the central premise of jihadi ideology, namely that jihad is the only solution to rid Muslims of their dictators; and the fact that the majority of the people in countries that underwent regime change are by their own choice embracing positive law through the electoral path: each of these circumstances emphasizes the irreconcilability of the jihadi worldview – which rejects the legitimacy of positive law – with that of the majority.

---

[43] The choice behind these figures is discussed in the introduction to this report.

The Jihadis' Challenges in the Wake of the Arab Spring

The Deed of Spectating

> It was inevitable for the revolution to happen regardless of how long it took, [its
> inevitability is established by] universal laws that we know from history,
> human knowledge and experiences ... [that is because] the accumulation of
> corruption that occurs in our umma, in our Arab and Islamic societies, cannot
> continue for long without it leading to a [socio-political] explosion ...
> nevertheless, like many people, I hadn't expected the revolution to happen this
> swiftly ... we thought, like many, that the people['s will to freedom] had died
> or [at least] they had become [politically] numb and for a long time to come ...[44]

The above statement was made by 'Atiyya in response to the Arab Spring. The early public
statements released by global jihadi leaders in reaction to the initial wave of the Arab Spring
reflected sincere rejoicing on their part: after all, the fall of Arab dictators is a dream, the
realization of which had originally set many jihadi leaders on the path of violent political action.
'Atiyya welcomed the revolutions with "enthusiasm and ardor"; Bin Ladin declared them to be
a "great historical event"; and early on Abu Yahya al-Libi and Ayman al-Zawahiri expressed
infinite pride in the *"thuwwar"* (revolutionaries) for rebelling against their dictators.

Yet the jihadis found themselves in an unprecedented situation: they had always prided
themselves on action, i.e., on the deed of jihad; and in so doing they gained the attention of the
world community. Furthermore, while the jihadis' actions did not correspond to successful
outcomes, such as establishing a global Islamic state or at least achieving unity among jihadis,
their actions nevertheless yielded decisive responses in so far as preoccupying the security
apparatuses of most states.[45] Thus, if, as Brian Jenkins artfully observes, "terrorism is theater,"
by which he means that "terrorism is aimed at the people watching [the terrorist attack], not at

---

[44] 'Atiyyatullah Abi 'Abd al-Rahman, "Thawrat al-Shu'ub wa-Suqut al-Nizam al-'Arabi al-Fasid," 16 February 2011, CTC Library.

[45] I am thinking of the nuanced distinctions Martha Crenshaw makes between "successful" and "effective" terrorism. See Martha Crenshaw, "The Effectiveness of Terrorism in the Algerian War," in Martha Crenshaw, ed., *Terrorism in Context*, University Park: Penn State Press, 2001.

the actual victims,"[46] then the post-9/11 decade must qualify as a decade of Oscar-quality performances by jihadis – or Tony-quality performances if limited to the theater.

At least during its initial stages, the Arab Spring robbed the jihadis of the attention to which they had become accustomed. Instead, global media and public attention turned to those whom the jihadis assumed, as 'Atiyya put it, to be politically "numb" and had lost the will to rebel against their oppressors. The people's weapon of choice was peaceful protest, the antithesis of what jihadis call for; what is more, when people power brought down the Presidents of Tunisia and Egypt, it proved to be more productive than jihad. Suddenly, the jihadis found themselves not as actors in, but as spectators of the drama of fallen dictators.

The deed of spectating was novel to jihadis. In a letter to 'Atiyya, Bin Ladin gave some credit to jihadis whose jihad in Afghanistan against the United States had, in his mind, consumed U.S. resources. Their jihad, he believed, weakened the United States "to such a degree that it enabled the Muslim people to reclaim some confidence and courage" and therefore rebel against the "agents of America," by which he meant their rulers.[47] Bin Ladin, however, did not include this view in his public response to the Arab Spring; instead, he gave full credit to the youth of Islam (*futyan al-Islam*) whose inspiration was not the jihadis, but the glorious era of their ancestors (*li-'ahdi ajdadihim*), in reference to the early Muslim community.[48]

Other global jihadi leaders were not as diplomatic as Bin Ladin; perhaps he could afford to display such sensitivity since he was killed soon after the onset of the Arab Spring and therefore did not face the pressure others experienced as they struggled to maintain the relevance of jihad. 'Atiyya devoted an entire statement to the matter, arguing among other things that al-Qa'ida contributed to the revolutions by "spreading the spirit of challenging and sustaining the power of rejecting and disdaining injustice," which, in his mind, assisted in breaking the hurdle of fear that had once gripped the masses and prevented them from rebelling against their

---

[46] Brian M. Jenkins, "International Terrorism: A New Kind of Warfare," The Rand Paper Series, June 1974, a PDF copy may be accessed on this link: http://www.rand.org/content/dam/rand/pubs/papers/2008/P5261.pdf (last accessed 4 August 2013), p. 4.
[47] SOCOM-2012-0000010, dated Monday, 22 Jumadi al-Awwal 1432 (25 April 2011).
[48] *Ibid.*

oppressors.[49] In a similar vein, al-Zawahiri applauds the pressure that the 9/11 attacks placed on the United States, which in his view caused it to "order" regimes in the region to "relax their grip on their people and the opposition," thereby leading to the rise of "popular anger" and a "volcanic explosion by the masses."[50] Other global jihadi leaders followed suit, using a variation of al-Zawahiri's assessment.[51]

"Jihad is the Only Solution" in Question

Serving as the spectators, instead of actors, in the drama that saw the fall of several Arab dictators, was only one of several challenges jihadis were forced to confront in the wake of the Arab Spring. More challenging for jihadi leaders was making the solution they had hitherto propagated – namely that "jihad is the only solution" to rid Muslims of their dictators – applicable to current events. Of course some jihadi groups were more sophisticated and strategic about implementing their jihadi solution than others.[52] To appreciate this challenge, it is important to place their premise in the context in which the jihadis reached such a radical position, the logical rationale that underpinned their premise,[53] and why the Arab Spring undermined it.

The political oppression that the people of the Middle East and North Africa have endured at the hands of autocratic regimes is a genuine grievance that motivated some Muslims to turn to jihad, believing it to be the only means of political change, thereby giving birth to the phenomenon of jihadism. Indeed, it is the radical nature of the response to this grievance that defines a jihadi and jihadism, as distinct from responses adopted by other political opposition forces. The approach of jihadi leaders and ideologues to this grievance was phrased in bleak

[49] 'Aiyya, "al-Thawrat al-'Arabiyya wa-Mawsim al-Hisad," CTC Library, August 2011.

[50] Ayman al-Zawahiri, "Fajru al-Nasri al-Washik," 14 September 2011, CTC Library.

[51] See also Abu Yahya al-Libi, "Khutbat 'Id al-Adha al-Mubarak li-'Am 1432," Dec. 2011; Adam Gadahn, "Ummat al-Tadhiya wa-al-Istishhad fi Muwajahat al-'Amala wa-al-Istibdad," Part 1, *Shabakat Ansar al-Mujahidin*, http:as-ansar.com/vb/showthread.php?t=79458 (last accessed 8 July 2013).

[52] Not all jihadi groups were pragmatic and strategic in their jihad: while al-Qa'ida is, others are driven by sectarianism and therefore their propagation of jihad does not enjoy the same level of plausibility. See, e.g., Brynjar Lia, *Architect of Global Jihad: the Life of al-Qaida Strategist Abu Mus'ab al-Suri*, New York: Columbia University Press, 2008; see also Nelly Lahoud, *Beware of Imitators: al-Qa'ida through the Lens of its Confidential Secretary*, CTC Report, June 2012.

[53] On the logic of terrorism, see Martha Crenshaw, "The Causes of Terrorism," *Comparative Politics*, Vol. 13, No. 4, July 1981.

terms and did not leave room for compromise: they argued that the dictators would never embrace genuine reform, nor would the democratic regimes in the West led by the United States and its allies permit such reforms. Convinced that the West's interests are best served by dictators in power, the jihadis repeatedly argue that democracy is a charade, or according to Bin Ladin, it is for "the white race only."[54] Jihad, they have asserted, is the only way out of this cul de sac, and positive law should be rejected in favor of Islamic Law if Muslims are to enjoy justice in this world.

Jihadi ideologues sought to popularize jihad by making it an individualized decision. In doing so, they rejected the legitimacy of the world order of nation-states and the state's monopoly on the use of violence within its own territory. This rejection was articulated as part of a broader theory of jihad that is nothing short of revolutionary, even though it did not lead to revolution. They drew on the classical corpus of the laws of war in Islam, and in particular on the doctrine of defensive jihad that stipulates that in the event that the territory/abode of Islam (*dar al-islam*) is invaded by non-Muslims, jihad becomes the individual obligation of every Muslim. But jihadi ideologues did not merely settle for territorial occupation as a condition for declaring jihad to be an individual obligation; they insisted that a land can qualify to be an abode of Islam only if its ruler and government adhere to Islamic principles of social justice. They went on to argue that Muslim countries today are run by dictators who serve the interests of non-Muslims; as such, these countries are for all intents and purposes occupied. Accordingly, there is no abode of Islam today, and it is the duty of Muslims to fight to create such an abode in which God's Law would reign supreme. Jihad, following this logic, is the individual obligation (*fard 'ayn*) of every Muslim.[55]

In view of this individualized and innovative understanding of the doctrine of defensive jihad, it stands to reason that those who translate it into action, namely the jihadis, undermine all

---

[54] Usama b. Ladin, "To The Americans," in *Messages to the World*, p. 169.

[55] Muhammad 'Abd al-Salam Faraj, executed in 1982 for his role in Anwar al-Sadat's assassination, was the first to advance this modern understanding of the legal defensive doctrine of jihad in his *al-Farida al-Gha'iba*. Global jihadis adopted it. See translation of Faraj's treatise by Johannes J. G. Jansen, *The Neglected Duty: The Creed of Sadat's Assassins and Islamic Resurgence in the Middle East*, New York: MacMillan Publishing Company, 1986, p. 200.

forms of political, religious and even parental authority.[56] As noted earlier, not only do such militants threaten the modern state's monopoly on the legitimate use of physical force, but they also threaten global security. Individualized jihad virtually became an ideological orthodoxy agreed upon by jihadis despite their differences.[57] This revolutionary view of jihad gained greater momentum through the various wars in which the United States and its allies fought in the territory of Muslim-majority states. Military intervention, followed by occupation and setting up what is termed "Western-friendly" regimes, unwittingly advanced the jihadi narrative. Since it is premised on a grievance that resonated with many, even those who are not in the jihadi fold or interested in pursuing a jihadi path, the jihadi narrative contributed a sense of credibility to their overall discourse.

Thus, notwithstanding the impossibility of ever achieving the idealistic goal of establishing a global Islamic state administered by divine justice, jihadi ideologues and leaders needed only to state what appeared to be obvious in order to vindicate their cause. While it is true that they did not give rise to the revolution of the peaceful "many" that the initial wave of the Arab Spring produced, they nevertheless instigated the revolt of the violent "few" and succeeded in changing the norms of personal liberties and freedoms in the context of delivering security in both democratic and non-democratic states, not least since the 9/11 attacks.

But the obvious political context that once supported the grievance narrative championed by jihadi leaders is not as obvious in the wake of the Arab Spring: that non-violent protest could sweep through the Middle East and North Africa and topple some of its iconic dictators like Husni Mubarak of Egypt and Zein al-'Abidin bin 'Ali of Tunisia is a direct challenge to the orthodoxy of the jihadi narrative. Furthermore, the initially peaceful nature of the protests and their success in ousting the dictators left little room for jihadis to serve as the agents of change. As spectators, they witnessed the realization of their dream realized by others, a fact they had to

---

[56] See Nelly Lahoud, "The Strength and Weaknesses of Jihadist Ideology", *CTC Sentinel*, vol. 3, Issue 10, 2010, pp.1-3.
[57] On ideological differences among jihadis, see Nelly Lahoud, *The Jihadis' Path to Self-Destruction*, New York/London: Columbia University Press/Hurst, 2010; see in particular the Introduction and Chapter Five. See also Lahoud, *Beware of Imitators: al-Qa'ida through the Lens of its Confidential Secretary*, CTC Report, 4 June 2012, pp. 37-41.

acknowledge, even while consoling themselves that it was the jihadis' heroism during previous decades that helped people to overcome their fears and enabled them to rise up against their dictators. In this light, does jihad as an individual obligation remain the only solution?

A related challenge is the jihadis' once apodictic contention that the West maintained unyielding support of Muslim dictators.[58] This claim is now disputed by the recent instance in which Western countries – including the United States – under the mandate of the United Nations launched a military campaign in support of Libyans seeking to bring down Mu'ammar al-Qadhafi's regime. It is noteworthy that jihadi leaders have grappled to present a coherent stance on the military intervention in Libya, with 'Atiyya evading the issue.[59] Nevertheless, regardless of the West's military intervention in support of people-power in Libya, and its in-principle support of the rebels in Syria, Western countries' current stance has not erased from people's memories the decades of support they had lent to now-fallen dictators. Jihadi leaders are using every opportunity to maintain these memories, reminding the people of the long-standing ties between Western democracies and Arab dictatorships.

From Grievances against Dictators to Resenting People's Embrace of Positive Law

Another challenge to the ideological framework the jihadis face in the wake of the Arab Spring is the seeming irrelevance of their message, as the majority of the people in Tunisia, Egypt and Libya embraced positive law (*qawanin wad'iyya*) through the electoral path as their means of political reform. Muslim voters, including parties running on Islamist and Salafi platforms, did not consider their participation in elections and their rhetorical commitment to building a democratic regime to compromise the tenets of their Islamic faith. However, jihadis outrightly reject the legitimacy of positive law, thereby declaring the political processes that govern the nation-state to be unlawful. These processes include the formation of political parties, contesting elections, and parliamentary systems. The jihadis' reasoning is littered with religious

---

[58] It should be noted that jihadis consider other non-Western powers, such as Iran, China and Russia, also to be their enemies, but their criticism of the West's support of dictators highlighted what the jihadis deem to be profound hypocrisy, particularly since it is the West that champions human rights, democracy, and the rule of law.
[59] In his "al-Thawrat al-'Arabiyya wa-Mawsim al-Hisad," released in August 2011, 'Atiyya, mentions in passing the NATO-led military intervention, without dwelling on it.

justification, arguing that since such processes are governed by man-made laws, they are in violation of God's Law.

Beyond religious justification, strategically oriented jihadis maintain that positive law should be rejected because the temptation to partake in the political processes of the nation-state is a recipe for abandoning jihad. They saw how Islamists were lured by the electoral path in pursuit of a democratic promise, inducing them to relinquish jihad. When Muhammad Mursi – the elected President of Egypt who resigned his membership of the Muslim Brotherhood (MB) before he assumed office – was ousted by the military in July 2013, al-Zawahiri was quick to remind the MB that their movement abandoned the commitment of its founder, Hasan al-Banna (d. 1949). Al-Banna's slogan was "jihad is our path; dying in the path of God is the highest desire [to which we long]"; the movement, according to al-Zawahiri, replaced this with "Islam is the solution" in order to enable involvement in the political process.[60] Al-Zawahiri maintains that in doing so the MB lost all: their religious principles and their right to govern. Al-Zawahiri overlooked Hasan al-Banna's decision to contest elections and declare himself a candidate on two occasions during his career.[61]

The jihadis' arguments against positive law and democracy were plausible when dictators reigned and elections were charades. The dynamics have changed in the aftermath of the Arab Spring: while Tunisia, Egypt and Libya are still far from qualifying as democracies, let alone as consolidated democracies,[62] people in these countries are at least rhetorically committed to democratic processes, and at most have demonstrated that commitment through participation

---

[60] Ayman al-Zawahiri, "Sanam al-'Ajwa al-Dimuqratiyya," *Shabakat al-Fida'*, August 2013, http://alfidaa.org/vb/showthread.php?t=71617 (last accessed 5 August 2013).

[61] Richard Mitchell, *The Society of the Muslim Brothers*, New York/Oxford: Oxford University Press, 1993, pp. 26-33. According to Mitchell, in 1942, al-Banna declared himself a candidate but withdrew his candidacy following the urging of Mustafa Nahhas Pasha, the head of the Wafd party. Al-Banna "consented, but 'at a price' which included (1) freedom for the movement to resume full-scale operations; and (2) a promise of government action against the sale of alcoholic drink and against prostitution," p. 27. In 1945, al-Banna and five MB members contested the elections, "believed to have been among the more obviously dishonest held in Egypt," and were all "defeated in constituencies where they had been certain of victory," p. 33. I owe this footnote to Brynjar Lia, one of the reviewers of this report.

[62] For the essential criteria of democracy, see Robert A. Dahl, "Polyarchy," *Toward Democracy: A Journey – Reflections: 1940–1997*, Volume 1, Berkeley: Institute of Government Studies Press, 1997, pp. 93-105, pp. 94-95; For a definition of consolidated democracy, see Juan J. Linz and Alfred Stepan, "Toward Consolidated Democracies," *Journal of Democracy*, Vol. 7, No. 2, 1996, p.16.

in elections: 52 percent of Tunisians turned out to vote in the October 2011 legislative elections; a similar proportion of Egyptians voted in the legislative elections in January and February 2012; and almost 62 percent of Libyans exercised their democratic prerogative in the legislative elections in July 2012.[63]

In view of the high voter turnout in these three countries, jihadi leaders are confronted with the reality that the majority of people made a clear and decisive choice, namely that they desire to forge a democratic path and that it does not undermine their faith. To an extent national political direction is now determined by citizens making their own choices. Despite the unrest that plagues Tunisia, Egypt and Libya, the "political game" (*al-lu'ba al-siyasiyya*) – the term used by jihadis to deride the political process – remains the dominant forum. Accordingly, the jihadis find themselves unable to partake in the political reforms of these countries. They remain out of the political game not through exclusion but by their own choice. Thus their once-powerful grievances articulated against dictators are now reduced to soliloquies criticizing the people who are embracing positive law and the international world order of nation-states. Realizing that they are not opposing the ideals of the "few," but rather of the majority of the population, jihadi leaders have chosen to remain ambiguous in their discourse as to the necessity of jihad, and in the meantime have failed to provide an alternative program likely to be adopted.

As the next chapter shows, the growing gap between the jihadi narrative and the people's grievances has naturally affected supporters of jihadism in countries that underwent regime change. The new jihadis in Tunisia, Egypt and Libya face a catch twenty-two dilemma: they are not disenfranchised, but they can only be "Shari'a-enfranchised" by disenfranchising the majority. The traditional jihadi response would be to rebel against the current governments. That is precisely what Ayman al-Zawahiri once advocated in unequivocal terms; in his mind, in Muslim countries, rulers whose source of governance relies on positive law are to be declared apostates: "it is the duty of Muslims to rebel against them, fight against them and oust them."[64] While this might have served jihadis during the time when the political establishment derived

---

[63] See *Election Guide*, http://www.electionguide.org/ (last accessed 4 November 2013).
[64] Ayman al-Zawahiri, *al-Hisad al-Murr*, p. 26.

its legitimacy only from authoritarianism, it is much less appealing in an era when governments derive legitimacy from the ballot box.

Jihadi Discourse: from Optimism to Pessimism

As will be discussed below, analysis of statements by global jihadi leaders reveals that the dramatic effects of the Arab Spring were not immediately felt in jihadi discourse. Due to ill-conception, isolation or simply wishful thinking, optimism was the jihadi leaders' initial response. But optimism was soon replaced with a sense of despair for those jihadi leaders who lived long enough to witness the growing irrelevance of their message, as people in Tunisia, Egypt and Libya cast their votes in their respective elections. It is in keeping with the calendar of the jihadis' changing outlook that the deaths of Bin Ladin and 'Atiyya within months of the onset of the Arab Spring preserve a sense of optimism in their statements, which display their attempts to carve out a participatory role for jihadis in the new era, with Bin Ladin highlighting the need to position the intellectually gifted jihadi leaders as public intellectuals who would guide public opinion.

If hope was on Bin Ladin's mind when he died, despair was most likely on Abu Yahya al-Libi's. Al-Libi, who tried hard to shift public opinion away from the democratic process, lived long enough to witness the declining appeal of the jihadi message. By the time he was killed in June 2012, the majority of people in countries that underwent regime change – including al-Libi's fellow Libyans – chose the ballot box. In the jihadis' mind, the people's choice amounted to rejection of the promise of the Shari'a's divine justice.

As Bin Ladin's declared successor, Ayman al-Zawahiri has inherited several unenviable tasks: when elections amounted to charades orchestrated by dictators, he could credibly argue for the illegitimacy of the democratic process and make a case for strict adherence to *tawhid*. How is he to make the same case now that the democratic process is the choice of the majority? And what guidance should he provide to his supporters in Tunisia, Egypt and Libya as he watches from a distance the new freedoms they now enjoy, in particular the freedom to embrace publicly the rhetoric of jihadism, but not to act on it?

Leaders of Global Jihad Respond

Usama Bin Ladin

The optimism and eloquence of Bin Ladin's response to the Arab Spring is a fitting point at which to begin to consider these questions. For many jihadis he represents the modern "sheikh al-Islam" and has now become, in their parlance, "the martyr of Islam – as we believe/hope for him to be" (*shahid al-islam – kama nahsabuhu*). Bin Ladin managed to compose only one relatively short public statement in response to the Arab Spring – no doubt due to the security measures he followed to prevent his capture or killing[65] – and it was released after his death.

If Bin Ladin's single public response is to be judged by the emotions it conveys, then it is indeed singular. The sentiments he expresses echo those of a private communication with 'Atiyya one week before his death, thereby corroborating its sincerity.[66] It is a highly moving statement, with parts of it composed of rhymed prose (*saja'*) and poetry. It is clear to him that the Arab world is undergoing a political transformation like no other, amounting to "a great historical event" (*hadath tarikhi 'azim*). "With the fall of the tyrant," he proudly asserts, "the meanings of submissiveness (*dhilla*), servility (*khunu'*), fear and restraint (*ihjam*) have [also] fallen," and the "meanings of freedom, dignity, courage and audacity (*iqdam*) have arisen."[67]

But if Bin Ladin's statement is to be judged by his own traditional discourse, which values the primacy of militancy as a force of change, then it reflects a significant shift away from advocating jihad. Indeed, noteworthy in Bin Ladin's response is his recognition of the uniqueness of the Arab Spring events, causing him to think in pragmatic and non-violent terms. While one might have expected him to compare the events with al-Qa'ida's signature achievements – e.g., the 1998 East Africa bombings that targeted the U.S. embassies in Nairobi and Dar al-Salam; the bombing assault on the USS Cole in 2000; and the 9/11 attacks – he made no such attempts. The noticeable absence of jihadi-related vocabulary in Bin Ladin's statement

---

[65] On Bin Ladin's security measures, see Liam Collins, "The Abbottabad Documents: Bin Ladin's Security Measures," *CTC Sentinel*, 22 May 2012.

[66] SOCOM-2012-0000010, dated Monday, 22 Jumadi al-Awwal 1432 (25 April 2011).

[67] Usama b. Ladin, "Kalimat Shahid al-Islam – Kama Nahsabuhu – li-Ummatihi al-Muslima," released by al-Sahab, May 19, 2011, CTC Library.

suggests that the events he was witnessing from his television screen signaled a new era for him; he speaks of a "decisive revolution" (*thawra masiriyya*) and at no point does he use the term "jihad." In this new parlance the movers of the Arab Spring are not designated as *mujahidun*, but as "free revolutionaries" (*thuwwar ahrar*) engaged in liberation (*tahrir*). He envisages a domino effect, observing that while Tunisia took the lead, soon "the knights of Egypt [carried the torch] of the free Tunisians [to light a fire] in Tahrir square, where a glorious revolution was launched, and what a revolution!"[68]

Bin Ladin recognized that the revolution was sparked by people's desire for freedom and dignity, and while he chose not to Islamize it, he was nevertheless keen to place the events and the actors in the context of Islamic history: "the youth of Islam," he asserts, "recalled into their minds the distinguished people [from Islamic history for their inspiration] and yearned for the [glorious] epoch of their ancestors." In other words, Bin Ladin sought to imbue the revolution with an Islamic character, hoping that the revolutionaries would forge a new path separate from the political processes that govern the world order: "you have a rare and great historical opportunity to raise the *umma* [to glory], and liberate yourselves from being in bondage to the whims of rulers, positive law and Western hegemony," he exhorted the revolutionaries. He went on to implore them not to squander this rare historical moment: "it would be a grave sin and dreadful ignorance to waste this opportunity that the *umma* had, for many decades, been awaiting; take advantage of it, destroy the idols and images and establish justice and faith."[69]

But what kind of an era did Bin Ladin envisage it to be and what type of strategy did he believe the new era demanded? It is with respect to devising a strategy to address the challenges brought about by the events that one vividly observes a development, one might even say an adjustment of gears, in Bin Ladin's thinking. For those who had closely followed Bin Ladin's public statements over the years, two points are compelling to highlight: the first has to do with the nature of his advice to youth; and the second has to do with the shift from his familiar tendency to favor an individualist/anarchic action to a collective action mediated by the learned.

---

[68] *Ibid.*
[69] *Ibid.*

With respect to youth, Bin Ladin's prior public statements had often called on youth, particularly those between the ages of fifteen and twenty-five,[70] to disregard those among the older generation who might dissuade them from taking up jihad. He even warned religious scholars who fear maintaining the banner of jihad and wish to abandon it "not [to] come between the youth of our umma and their jihad for the sake of God."[71] In these older public statements Bin Ladin was in the habit of encouraging the youth to take up militancy with or without the approval of the political or religious authorities: "If individual jihad is an obligation upon our entire umma today," he said in one of his speeches, "then it is even more so for the youth than it is for the old."[72]

By contrast, Bin Ladin's post-Arab Spring statement urges the youth not to take decisive actions without consultation with the experts and the learned, stressing that the opinion of the learned should take precedence over the courage of the brave (*al-ra'y qabla shaja'at al-shuj'an*). This is a remarkable departure from Bin Ladin's jihadi mode. It is as if the Arab Spring flipped the dynamics of action in his mind from an individualist, even anarchic form of violence to a collective non-violent action guided by the wisdom of the learned.

There is more to Bin Ladin's new focus on the learned guidance of the young. As discussed in the introduction, jihadi ideology suffers from a tension between the egalitarianism that it grants to its adherents on the battlefield and the elitism it promotes as part of governance. Global jihadi leaders have not had to deal with governance, nor did they need to theorize about it. They simply relied on a pre-modern view of governance that privileged the educated elites, thereby allowing them to lionize the masses without showing contempt for them. Even though the Arab Spring did not open the door for jihadis to govern, it nevertheless forced them to accommodate the possibility that jihad and non-violence both had to be entertained as means of political change.

---

[70] Usama b. Ladin, in Bruce Lawrence (ed.), *Messages to the World*, p. 91.
[71] *Ibid.*, p. 201.
[72] *Ibid.*, p. 203.

It is in this spirit that Bin Ladin quickly realized that the next battle the jihadis face is not one with dictators and is not one that involves jihad. It is rather a battle of persuading the people who in his view ought to be educated in the "proper understanding of Islam."[73] He advises that "it is a legal obligation to establish a council that would provide advice and counsel to the Muslim people pertaining to all pivotal matters." He calls on scholars who earned credibility with the people on account of having a long history of opposing the regimes to establish such a council and even create an:

> … operation room to accompany the events and provide balanced responses to address the needs of the umma. At the same time, [the council should] take advantage of the proposals put forward by people of understanding/educated elites (*uwlu al-nuhan*) in this umma and seek the assistance of qualified research centers and leading public intellectuals. [They should all endeavor] to support the peoples who are struggling to bring down their tyrants and whose sons are being killed and [also] to guide those who managed to bring down their rulers and part of the [regime] apparatus with the desired [future] steps to protect the revolution and realize its objectives.[74]

In his letter to 'Atiyya, Bin Ladin is not as optimistic as to the feasibility of establishing the council he calls for in his public statement and recommends that the *mujahidun* should fill this gap. In other words, he proposes giving a new vocation to the literarily gifted among al-Qa'ida's leaders; they were to be transformed from leaders of jihad to *public* intellectuals of *da'wa*. While recognizing the many duties they shoulder, he nevertheless believed that "this great duty [of advising the umma] should occupy the biggest portion of our efforts" and that this entailed "calling upon all those with literary capabilities, gifted with rhetorical eloquence, be it prose or poetry, to deliver [statements] as audio, visual or in writing."[75] In practical terms, he wanted to launch a massive media campaign; he asked 'Atiyya to spare none of the literarily

---

[73] SOCOM-2012-0000010.
[74] Usama b. Ladin, "Kalimat Shahid al-Islam."
[75] SOCOM-2012-0000010 .

gifted leaders and direct them to "incite people who have not yet revolted and exhort them to rebel against the rulers."[76]

Bin Ladin anticipated – correctly – that countries undergoing revolutions would elect Islamist parties into government. Such an outcome, of course, is not the ideal scenario Bin Ladin envisages for the *umma* at large. Consistent with his prior views, he believed the Islamists were those who favored "half solutions" (*ansaf al-hulul*), but he did not think that this was the time to confront them. He urged 'Atiyya to warn jihadi "brothers" in countries undergoing revolution to avoid conflicts with Islamist parties. It is likely that Bin Ladin was counting on the failures of Islamist parties in government to discredit them in the eyes of the public; in the meantime "our obligation during this period is to focus on *da`wa* (missionary activities, particularly preaching) among Muslims and win supporters by spreading the proper understanding [of Islam]."[77] Observers of Egyptian politics may argue that the fate of the Muslim Brotherhood in Egypt is a vindication of Bin Ladin's assessment.

Unlike other global jihadi leaders, Bin Ladin did not show resentment toward the people in his public or his private statements. In these documents he appears confident that the democratic phase would ultimately fail; that is why "if we double our efforts towards guiding, educating and warning Muslim people from those [who might tempt them to settle for] half solutions, by carefully presenting [our] advice, then the next phase will [witness a victory] for Islam, if God so pleases."[78] To be fair to other jihadi leaders who could not hide their resentment of the people in their public statements, Bin Ladin did not live long enough to experience the negligible influence of his message. Ironically, the timing of his death spared him the experiences his fellow jihadi leaders faced when their admonitions fell on deaf ears. With his new emphasis on guidance and preaching as a strategy, he, like other jihadi leaders, would have struggled with the military intervention in Libya and the divisions that have arisen among jihadis as a result of the fighting in Syria (see Conclusion).

---

[76] SOCOM-2012-0000010.
[77] SOCOM-2012-0000010.
[78] *Ibid.*

'Atiyyatallah al-Libi

Judging by the declassified documents recovered from Bin Ladin's compound in Abbottabad, most of Bin Ladin's correspondence was processed through 'Atiyya, at least during the latter part of 2010 and until his death in May 2011. In view of the dates on which 'Atiyya's public statements were released, the news of the events of the Arab Spring reached him before they did Bin Ladin.[79] It was a U.S. drone strike that killed 'Atiyya in North Waziristan in August 2011.[80] According to Ayman al-Zawahiri's eulogy, 'Atiyya spent the last night of his life "following the news of the conquest of Tripoli at the hands of his jihadi brethren."[81] Al-Zawahiri may have been adding his own rhetorical flourish here, but it is true that some of 'Atiyya's public statements following the Arab Spring were filled with an optimistic enthusiasm that envisaged a participatory role for jihadis in the new era. Nevertheless, he was careful to stress the limitations of the organization: "al-Qa'ida does not have a magic wand as some believe … it is but a small part of the larger efforts exerted by the *umma* that is struggling [to reclaim its rights]; therefore, do not expect from al-Qa'ida more than it can deliver."[82] Like Bin Ladin, 'Atiyya emphasized the need to focus on *da'wa* to instill what he deems to be a proper foundation of Islamic education and governance, away from positive law but without coming into conflict with Islamist groups.[83] Also, like Bin Ladin, he was killed before the political transitions that clearly demonstrated the desire of the majority of the people in Libya, Tunisia and Egypt for change through the electoral process. With hindsight, his optimism was unrealistic.

'Atiyya was initially overjoyed to receive news of the fall of several dictators. It must have delighted him to quote several verses composed by the renowned Iraqi writer of revolutionary poetry, Ahmad Matar, in which he ridicules dictators. Matar envisaged the fate of dictators as

---

[79] In all likelihood, documents and correspondence in 'Atiyya's home base would have been a treasure trove as far as insight into al-Qa'ida's recent inner workings are concerned. This is unlike the killing of Bin Ladin, which involved the presence of Special Operations Forces (SOF) who collected materials from the compound. See discussion in *Letters from Abbottabad: Bin Ladin Sidelined?* CTC Report, 3 May 2012, pp. 8-9.

[80] "Al-Qaida's Number two Killed in Pakistan," *The Guardian*, 27 August 2011, http://www.theguardian.com/world/2011/aug/27/al-qaida-two-killed-pakistan

[81] Ayman al-Zawahiri, "Risalat al-Amal wa-al-Bishr li-Ahlina fi Misr (8)," CTC Library.

[82] 'Atiyyatullah, "Thawrat al-Shu'ub wa-Suqut al-Nizam al-'Arabi al-Fasid," 16 February 2011, CTC Library.

[83] *Ibid.*

ultimately one that is decided by the crowd, who will accept nothing less than turning the body of the dictator into the sole of a boot on which to stamp their feet, a fate not unlike that which befell Qadhafi. In Matar's words:

> I recognize that rhyme
>
> Cannot by itself the tyrant's throne bring down
>
> But I can still use it to tan his skin like the hide of cattle they brand
>
> So that when, through a decisive blow, his time has come
>
> And from the hands of the barefooted crowd [his fallen body I rush to] grab
>
> Into [their] shoes, his branded hide would be ready to be turned.[84]

Beyond rejoicing at the fall of dictators, the Arab Spring seems to have brought out a nationalist fervor in 'Atiyya. Jihadism, it should be remembered, is opposed to nationalism as an extension of its rejection of the legitimacy of the nation-state. It disdains what it considers to be the segregationist nature of nationalism that divides people with artificial borders.

In his second statement, also released during February 2011, 'Atiyya adopts a careless nationalist tone. By then, the winds of political change had reached his native homeland, where his fellow Libyans took to the street, seeking to bring down Qadhafi. 'Atiyya does not restrain himself, imprudently revealing emotions that are unmistakably nationalist, projecting an alternative picture of Libya to that displayed by an obtuse Qadhafi, whose speeches were mocked by the international media.[85] It is as if 'Atiyya were seeking to position himself as a spokesperson for Libyans. Qadhafi, he states, "embarrassed us [as Libyans] before the world!" He continues: "I wish to apologize to all Arabs and Muslims with regard to what originated from this deranged, pharaonic and doomed to perdition [Qadhafi], I apologize to the free ones and to those who espouse independent [political views], such as jurists/lawyers and others; [I also apologize] to journalists from al-Jazeera and other [media outlets], and I apologize to those

---

[84] Cited in *Ibid*. I recognize that my translation does not convey the powerful meaning of the original Arabic; Arabists are urged to read it in the original.

[85] See for example his February 2011 speech, http://www.youtube.com/watch?v=69wBG6ULNzQ (last accessed 28 May 2013).

who respect intellect, literature and honor; [I beg all of you to erase] the [image] that this corrupt [Qadhafi represents and which] distorts Libya and its people."[86]

'Atiyya displays an over-confident tone and a cavalier optimism in his first two statements. His proclamation that "the post-Qadhafi era is unquestionably the era of Islam" was at best misguided, not least since the various contenders, including the former jihadi 'Abd al-Hakim Belhaj, rushed to embrace the electoral process to pursue a democratic path.[87] They formed political parties and contested the election in July 2012, which saw the victory of the National Forces Alliance, a party that ran on a secular platform.[88] Indeed, to-date Libya has been the only country to undergo regime change as a result of the Arab Spring and did not elect an Islamist party.

By contrast to his earlier statements in response to the Arab Spring, 'Atiyya's last two statements – released in the same month that he was killed – were void of optimism. He must have sensed by then that the jihadis' worldview was going to be difficult to reconcile with that of many people. He devoted one statement to making a case for the continued relevance of jihadism, responding to analysts and commentators who argued that the peaceful protesters in the MENA region achieved in weeks what jihadis failed to achieve in decades.

The proposition that the Arab Spring highlighted the failure of jihadism by proving that the weapon of peaceful protest was more successful than jihad troubled all jihadi leaders and engendered defensive and often resultantly fallacious responses. 'Atiyya struggled to present an internally coherent response: on the one hand, he argued that the revolutions cannot be said to be entirely peaceful, pointing to incidents of violence where people attacked police stations, and to clashes between protesters and security forces. In citing these petty instances he is at

---

[86] 'Atiyya, "Tahiyya li-Ahlina fi Libya," February 2011, CTC Library.

[87] On Belhaj's commitment to the democratic process, see Umar Khan, "I'm a civilian, LIFG is history; I want an apology not the money," *Libya Herald*, 2 June 2012, http://www.libyaherald.com/2012/06/02/im-a-civilian-lifg-is-history-i-want-an-apology-not-the-money-belhaj/ (last accessed 28 May 2013).

[88] David Kirpatrick, Election Results in Libya Break an Islamist Wave," 8 July 2012, *The New York Times*, http://www.nytimes.com/2012/07/09/world/africa/libya-election-latest-results.html?pagewanted=all&_r=0 (last accessed 28 May 2013); See also, "Libya election success for secularist Jibril's bloc," *BBC*, 18 July 2012, http://www.bbc.co.uk/news/world-africa-18880908 (last accessed 28 May 2013).

pains to defend the premise of jihad and its ongoing validity to the Arab Spring, suggesting that the jihadis and the protesters are part of the same enterprise. On the other hand, he distinguishes the objective of the protesters from that of al-Qa'ida, remarking that unlike the partial and tactical objectives of the revolution that characterizes the Arab Spring, al-Qa'ida seeks "a radical and a genuine revolutionary change, the objective of which is to make God's Word reign supreme."[89] Perhaps fearing the charge that he might be suffering from attention deficit, he contradicts himself further by concluding that the jihadis "were overjoyed by these revolutions, they supported them and considered them to be complementing their work and objectives."[90]

Undoubtedly, the military intervention in Libya mandated by the UN and led by NATO would have been on 'Atiyya's mind, even though he chose to remark on it only briefly, observing that it was a "predicament" (*warta*).[91] Indeed, the intervention in Libya was intended to protect civilians, including the provision of support for those who became rebels, the very people 'Atiyya was saluting in his earlier statements. The rebels and the NATO-led forces together brought down the regime and caused Qadhafi and his family to flee; Qadhafi was captured and killed in October 2011. In his other statement released in August, 'Atiyya chose to address his attention to the jihadis, perhaps fearing that they would be tempted to abandon jihad and join the revolutionaries. In this statement he speaks of a "tree of jihad," assuring his fellow jihadis that while "the path of jihad is long and arduous, it tastes sweet to those who have savored the sweetness of the faith." It is as if he feels compelled to remark positively on the revolutions, noting in passing that they "broke the hurdle of fear" that had paralyzed Arab people in the face of their dictators; but even this brief remark is qualified: he adds that "the current image of the revolutions is, without a doubt, not the image that is desired or hoped for."[92]

'Atiyya's onset of despair was to be magnified by those who inherited the torch of jihadi leadership, namely Abu Yahya al-Libi and Ayman al-Zawahiri. Al-Zawahiri initially enjoyed

---

[89] 'Aiyya, "al-Thawrat al-'Arabiyya wa-Mawsim al-Hisad Hasad?"
[90] *Ibid.*
[91] *Ibid.*
[92] 'Atiyya, "Basha'ir al-Narsr fi Shahr al-Sabr," 30 August 2011, CTC Library.

and projected a certain optimism resulting from the Arab Spring, but before long found himself struggling to deliver an internally coherent jihadi message.

Abu Yahya al-Libi

Abu Yahya al-Libi is a distinguished jihadi orator known for his rich Arabic vocabulary and eloquence. His death in June 2012 must have pained many surviving jihadi leaders, not just because of al-Libi's prolific contributions to jihadi ideology, but also because their possible deaths in battle will not be commemorated by al-Libi in one of his many elaborate and distinct eulogies. Such writings are not merely about celebrating the death and martyrdom of fallen jihadi leaders – they also demonstrate to living leaders the way in which they too will be memorialized.

Given al-Libi's literary gift, it is no surprise that Bin Ladin singled his name out in his letter to 'Atiyya as one of those with "literary capabilities" who should be central to the massive media campaign advising the *umma* in the wake of the Arab Spring.[93] But al-Libi had already taken the initiative when, almost seven weeks before Bin Ladin composed his letter to 'Atiyya, he had released the first of several public statements in response to the recent revolutionary events.

When al-Libi released his first statement on 13 March 2011, he, like Bin Ladin, was filled with optimism. As its title suggests, his statement was addressed to "Our People in Libya"; by then, Libyans had taken to the streets, following the example of Tunisians and Egyptians whose protests brought down Zayn al-Din bin 'Ali of Tunisia and Husni Mubarak. Al-Libi must have feared that Libyans might be intimidated since, unlike Tunisia and Egypt, the government of Qadhafi used airstrikes to quell protests. His statement was intended to boost morale, reminding Libyans of the oppression they endured during Qadhafi's reign and congratulating them on rising up against tyranny "following the example of their heroic neighbors and for reviving the heroic epic of their fearless ancestors."[94] He called on Libyans to commit their lives to the revolution: "there is no room for half solutions," he asserts, "and death is to be

---

[93] SOCOM-2012-0000010.
[94] Abu Yahya al-Libi, "Ila Ahlina fi Libya," 13 March 2011, CTC Library.

experienced but once," reminding them of the powerful verses composed by the great tenth-century poet al-Mutanabbi, which most native Arabs know by heart:

> If you risk your life in pursuit of a glorious goal
>
> Do not settle for anything short of [reaching] the stars
>
> For the taste of death in pursuit of a small goal
>
> Is the same as that in pursuit of a glorious one

As one might expect of a jihadi leader, al-Libi did not miss injecting an anti-American flavor into his statement, no doubt concerned that Libyans might respond to the sympathies that many Western governments, including the United States, displayed in support of the revolutions. He therefore reminds them of the decades of U.S. support enjoyed by Mubarak's regime, dubbing it the "Husni-Barack" regime to highlight the marriage of interests between Arab dictators and the United States, including Barack Obama's administration.[95] By the time al-Libi released further statements, the United States along with other European countries under the UN mandate had launched a military campaign in support of the Libyan people, assisting the rebels in their fight against the Qadhafi regime's violent response to their initial peaceful demonstrations. Al-Libi was shrewd enough to know that NATO's air campaign was critical to the military defeat of Qadhafi's regime. But this did not alter his perception of Western powers; the West, he believes, was not in the habit of putting Arab people's wellbeing ahead of its own interests:

> It is well known to anyone with [even half] a brain that the reason Western
>
> states like France, Britain, America and those that support them intervened
>
> with their airpower [in Libya] was not to protect the red blood, the blood of
>
> civilians, as they claim. Rather, they intervened out of concern that [they may
>
> lose control over] the black blood, i.e., oil, that nourishes their economies and
>
> injects life into their industries.[96]

---

[95] Abu Yahya al-Libi, "Ila Ahlina fi Libya," 13 March 2011, CTC Library.
[96] Abu Yahya al-Libi, "Libya Madha Yuradu laha?," October 2011, CTC Library.

As it became clearer that people driving the Arab Spring were calling for the application of the rule of law through the formation of political parties and the institution of electoral processes, al-Libi's initial optimism declined. His subsequent statements were as much addressed to the jihadis as they were to the "revolutionaries" (*thuwwar*), lest the jihadis would be tempted – or as al-Libi would suggest, deluded – by calls for a democratic solution. One passing reference in Bin Ladin's letter to 'Atiyya dated April 2011 suggests that some jihadis may have been too eager, perhaps unstoppably so, to leave the Pakistan–Afghanistan region to partake in the revolutions.[97] Al-Libi may well have had such jihadis in mind when he remarks, also in April 2011 that:

> Given that the events are of such magnitude and their torrential flow is moving
> with force towards [political] change to the unknown through bringing down
> the regimes, it is necessary for the jihadis to take a stance and make their views
> known about these events. [They would do so] holding firm to the steadfast
> principles of their blessed jihadi path while profiting in so far as it is possible
> from these major and consecutive changes. [In this way] they would not miss
> out on available opportunities [to advance their agenda] without being
> ardently, emotionally or enthusiastically carried away by the calls for change,
> those that lack insight and careful examination.[98]

As far as al-Libi was concerned, the Arab world had witnessed dramatic political changes, including numerous military coups whose leaders promised, through "fiery speeches," victories that never materialized. The *umma*, he believes, had already experienced severe disappointment when its "heroic leaders proved to be nothing but submissive traitors, agents [of] and slaves [to

---

[97] SOCOM-2012-0000010, p. 6. After the capture of the al-Qa'ida operative (Abu) Anas al-Libi in Libya, one jihadi website posted photographs of al-Libi being involved in the public life of Libya post-Arab Spring, indicating that he had lost his son during the conflict. The photographs show him distributing prizes and speaking in public: "al-Hiwar al-Siyasi al-Libi," *Shabakat al-Fida'*, 8 October 2013, http://alfidaa.org/vb/showthread.php?t=77445 (accessed the same day). See also "Profile: Anas al-Liby," *BBC*, 7 October 2003 http://www.bbc.co.uk/news/world-africa-24418327 (accessed the same day).

[98] Abu Yahya al-Libi, "Thawrat al-Shu'ub: bayna al-Ta'aththur wa-al-Ta'thir," p. 6.

Western imperial powers]."[99] He feared that the furor of the Arab Spring would prove to be an empty vessel – that which promises nothing but makes the most sound.

If the false revolutions of the past gave birth to tyrants, al-Libi's concern this time was the falsehood engendered by the people themselves. His statements were much less tactful than those of Bin Ladin, exhibiting resentful sentiments towards the very people whose audience he was seeking. For example, he could not hide his wonder that the people of the region were for decades unmoved by the regimes of the dictators against whom they were now rebelling, leaving the jihadis to shoulder the burden of the political struggle on their own. The jihadis' lonely efforts, he held, felt as if they were "sculpting a stone with their nails." He did not ask explicitly for gratitude, but he wanted it to be known that the jihadis had made too many sacrifices to remain empty-handed (*safqat al-maghbun*).[100]

Although al-Libi continued to pay the people compliments for having "overcome their fears" and shown courage in rising up against their dictators, he could not understand how they could fall prey to the imposters (*ahl al-dajal*), those who make them "silly" (*tafahat*) promises of delivering "democracy, plurality, freedom of speech and expression." After all, how could they not know that "God's religion is about the unity of this umma … while the religion of democracy is about shredding the Islamic umma in the name of plurality. [Look at] Tunisia today after this revolution, it has more than 81 political parties, 81 political parties?!"[101] Are the people then as "silly" as the promises they believe in al-Libi's mind? While he may not explicitly state it, his sentiments certainly suggest that he believes them to be forging something akin to an idiocracy.

An overall assessment of al-Libi's statements reveals that he was conflicted regarding the revolutions. On the one hand, he wanted the revolutions to expand and released a statement inciting the Algerian people, reminding them of their revolutionary past and calling on them to

---

[99] *Ibid.*, p. 11.
[100] *Ibid.*, p. 6.
[101] Abu Yahya al-Libi, "Khutbat 'Id al-Adha al-Mubarak li-'Am 1432," Dec. 2011. The *Partis Tunisie* website lists 110 political parties in Tunisia. See *Partis Tunisie* (Arabic and French), http://www.partistunisie.com/fr/Tous_les_partis.html (last accessed 29 May 2013).

rebel,[102] a call Algerians by and large blithely ignored. On the other hand, al-Libi's despair at the outcome of the revolutions is unmistakable:

> I compare what has happened today to our oppressed and tyrannized people to that of a prisoner whose hands and ankles have been shackled for a long time and locked in a room by himself where he is not allowed to talk; he cannot see the light except for the occasional rays that penetrate the holes of his cell's small window and quickly fade[103] ... Suddenly, this prisoner is moved from his depressing situation, deadly solitude and frightening desolation into a [different] room [where he is put] with a group of people. In [this] room, he is together with a number of 'free prisoners' inside their roomy prison cell; he sees the light, converses with his friends for as long as he wishes, and performs the communal prayer with them ... Inside this new room then, there is light, conversing is permitted and [physical] movement is possible, except that the truth that could not be denied or buried about this prisoner's situation is that he remains a prisoner with all that this description entails. At best, what happened [to him] is that he moved from one [small] prison [cell] into a more spacious one.[104]

Al-Libi nevertheless had something from the Arab Spring for which to be thankful, which is the death of Qadhafi. Remarking on Qadhafi's 42-year rule over Libya, al-Libi consolingly reflects that "I entered this world and I saw Qadhafi in front of me, but praise be to God, I have not departed until he himself exited it."[105] It is of course a coincidence that the U.S. drone strike that killed al-Libi on June 2012 in North Waziristan was timed to meet his wishes.[106]

---

[102] Abu Yahya al-Libi, "al-Jaza'ir wa-Ma'rakat al-Sabr," October 2011, CTC Library.

[103] Abu Yahya al-Libi's Arabic is superb and virtually flawless, but this specific aspect of the metaphor is weak: one would expect the 'holes' through which the prisoner could experience light to be in the wall of the room but not part of a window; otherwise, the light would get through the entire glass window.

[104] Abu Yahya al-Libi, "Thawrat al-Shu'ub: bayna al-Ta'aththur wa-al-Ta'thir," Tala'i' Khurasan, April/May 2011, pp. 7-8 (Issue 17, Rabi' al-Thani); it was posted on 1 May 2011 on *Shabakat Shumukh al-Islam*.

[105] Abu Yahya al-Libi, "Khutbat 'Id al-Adha al-Mubarak li-'Am 1432 h.," December 2011, CTC Library.

[106] Declan Walsh and Eric Schmitt, "Drone Strike Killed No. 2 in Al Qaeda, U.S. Officials Say," *The New York Times*, 5 June 2012, http://www.nytimes.com/2012/06/06/world/asia/qaeda-deputy-killed-in-drone-strike-in-pakistan.html?pagewanted=all (last accessed 28 May 2013).

Ayman al-Zawahiri

After the killings of Bin Ladin, 'Atiyya and al-Libi, the policy world now turns to Ayman al-Zawahiri as the global leader of jihad, regardless of his control or otherwise of the jihadi landscape. As such, al-Zawahiri has the unenviable task not only of commenting on the rapidly evolving political transformations brought about by the Arab Spring, but also of projecting coherence and integrity onto a global jihadi scene that is more than ever divided. In view of the complex and unpredictable challenges he is facing, al-Zawahiri's public statements in response to the Arab Spring have understandably suffered from a lack of a consistent vision; and his supporters, the "new jihadis," in countries that underwent regime change, are embodying this inconsistency (see chapter two). Worse still, if the political change in Tunisia, Egypt and Libya has sidelined jihadism and disrupted al-Zawahiri's ideological and political agenda and once tenacious edge, the situation in Syria, which might have restored the credibility of the doctrine that jihad is the only solution, is also challenging al-Zawahiri's leadership. As the concluding chapter of this report explains, in view of what appears to be irreconcilable public differences between the Islamic State of Iraq (and the Levant) and Jabhat al-Nusra,[107] the jihadis are snatching derision from the jaws of credibility and al-Zawahiri is the global leader getting the credit/blame for it.

Al-Zawahiri's public statements since the onset of the Arab Spring have canvassed many issues concerning different aspects of worldly affairs. His response to the Arab Spring has been largely – though not exclusively – addressed in the series of audio and video recordings entitled "Missive of Hope and Joy to our People in Egypt."[108] The first statement in the series suggests that he had begun preparing it before the unfolding of the events that came to define the Arab Spring; it seems that he had intended the series to present an historical account of Western encroachments on Egypt. He refers to Napoleon's invasion of Egypt in the eighteenth century,

---

[107] On renaming the Islamic State of Iraq, see concluding chapter.

[108] Ayman al-Zawahiri, "Risalat al-Amal wa-al-Bishr li-Ahlina fi Misr," CTC Library. At the time of writing this report he had released a total of eleven audio and visual recordings in this series. For detailed analysis of the first five statements, see Nelly Lahoud, "Ayman al-Zawahiri's Reaction to Revolution in the Middle East," *CTC Sentinel*, 1 April 2011.

followed by the British occupation in the nineteenth and early twentieth centuries, and in recent history he argues that the United States exercises indirect rule over Egypt through Muslim dictators or, in jihadi parlance, the "Pharaohs," who have served as agents of the United States. Even though he changes emphasis in subsequent statements in order to address current events, he returns to the historical theme in a later recording in the series (*Missive 7*), perhaps because he wanted to make use of material that he had prepared earlier.

During the first few months of the revolutions the tone of al-Zawahiri's statements is optimistic. It is clear to him that *al-tali'a al-jihadiyya* (jihadi vanguards) no longer hold a virtual monopoly as the Muslim world's drivers of political change, but he did not hesitate to salute the protesters, the "free and the noble people (*al-ahrar wa-al-shurafa'*)" (*Missive 3*). While he recognizes that the protesters are not one and the same with the jihadis, he is keen to combine them all in the same camp, fighting the same enemy: "your jihadi brethren are confronting alongside you the same enemy, America and its Western allies, those who set up [tyrants] like Husni Mubarak, Zein al-'Abidin b. 'Ali, 'Ali 'Abdallah Saleh, 'Abdallah b. Hussein and their ilk to rule over you (*sallatu*)" (*Missive 4*). To highlight his approval or perhaps establish a common bond between him and the protesters, he noted that before emigrating from Egypt "I used to be diligent about participating in popular demonstrations" first against Nasser's regime, then against Sadat's (*Missive 6*).

He was deliberate in focusing on the United States, cautioning the people of Egypt not to be deceived by the current U.S. support of their cause. He reminds them that:

> [America] that is [now] weeping over the safety of journalists in Egypt [is the same America] that bombed the offices of *al-Jazira* in Kabul and Baghdad ... America that is [now] weeping over the victims of torture in Egypt is [the same America] that resorts to torture in the prisons of Guantanamo, Bagram and Abu Ghraib and in its secret prisons in Egypt, Jordan, Morocco, Poland and on board of its ships and airplanes ... this is the truth of the international legal system ... it is the law that [enshrines] the domination of the arrogant (*mustakbirin*) [of the earth] over the disinherited (*mustad'afin*). America that weeps over the [deficit]

of democracy [in the Middle East] is [the same America] that refuses to recognize the [elected] government of Hamas in Gaza and the West Bank. America is the last [entity] that is allowed to speak of [the virtues of] democracy and human rights (*Missive 5*).

Beyond highlighting what he deems to be the hypocrisy of the United States and its allies, al-Zawahiri warns the people of Egypt that the fruits of their revolution may be squandered if they do not institute an Islamic government premised on the principle of consultation (*nizam islami shuri*). More specifically, he calls for the abrogation of the constitution and establishing in its place an Islamic system of government free of positive law (*Missive 5*), and gives detailed analysis concerning why the constitution of Egypt is in violation of the Shari'a (*Missive 6*).

The situation in Libya had the potential to provide al-Zawahiri with the opportunity to return jihad to prominence; he may have also hoped that his call on the Yemenis and Algerians to rise up might make more room for jihad if al-Qa'ida in the Arabian Peninsula (AQAP) and al-Qa'ida in the Islamic Maghreb (AQIM) could join in. That is perhaps why he released a statement addressed specifically to Yemen in which he capitalized on the cosmetic transition from 'Ali 'Abdallah Salih to his deputy 'Abd Rabbu Mansour Hadi, accusing the latter of being as subservient to U.S. interests as his predecessor. The recording of the statement also includes excerpts from one of Anwar al-'Awlaqi's lectures, denouncing U.S. involvement in Yemen.[109] Al-Zawahiri misread the situation: Yemen and Algeria did not yield a violent battlefield, and he wrongly assumed that Western intervention would rally people to fight against NATO forces, as he urged them to do (*Missive 5*).

It must have surprised al-Zawahiri to see the popular Libyan support for military intervention, and he found himself explaining bitterly that NATO is not a "charitable institution," but an alliance of the most arrogant of world powers (*mustakbirin*) whose intent is to rob Libya of its natural resources and turn it into another Iraq. He urged Libyans to store light and heavy weaponry and to organize military training courses, erroneously envisaging a protracted

---

[109] Ayman al-Zawahiri, "al-Yaman bayna 'Amilin Dhahib wa-'Amilin Na'ib," May 2012, CTC Library.

violent conflict there, proclaiming that "the battle in Libya is the battle of the Islamic umma" (*Missive 6*). Despite the fact that, unlike Tunisia and Egypt, it took a violent conflict to bring down Libya's dictator, it still did not prove to be the battlefield that al-Zawahiri hoped it would be.

Has al-Zawahiri made any gains in countries that underwent regime change? As far as events on the ground, al-Zawahiri has flirted with groups operating in the Gaza–Sinai region (see chapter two). He applauded those who repeatedly attacked the Egypt–Israel gas pipelines, and the attackers, in turn, dedicated these offensives to al-Zawahiri (*Missive 8*). Since the elections of the Islamist parties in Tunisia (Hizb al-Nahda) and Egypt (Muslim Brotherhood), al-Zawahiri has taken every opportunity to highlight what he believes to be an inconsistency between the Islamic agenda these parties project in their names and rhetoric and their policy and actions which, he suggests, equates to hypocrisy. For example, when Hizb al-Nahda won the October 2011 election in Tunisia and declared that the party would not seek to make the Shari'a the source of legislation,[110] al-Zawahiri's response was imbued with sarcasm. Fond of analogies, especially medical ones, he asked:

> Have you ever heard that a hospital declares that it has nothing to do with attending to curing the sick, or a pharmacy stating that it has nothing to do with selling medications or an army positing that it has nothing to do with fighting … or a democratic or secular group proclaiming that it does not seek to apply [democracy or secularism]? … They [i.e., Islamist parties] are but a symptom of our [modern] civilizational illnesses … they are creating an Islam that has the approval of the U.S. Department of State, the European Union and the Gulf Sheikhs.[111]

Yet, beyond his clever and acerbic criticism, as far as Tunisia, Egypt and Libya are concerned, al-Zawahiri has had little to offer by way of vision. He shifted his once activist "jihad is the only

---

[110] The party won 90 of the 217 seats in Parliament, see http://www.aawsat.com/details.asp?section=4&article =647331&issueno=12023; Rashid al-Ghannushi, http://www.youtube.com/watch?v=osHZMqbRJOI& feature=related (last accessed 28 May 2013).
[111] Ayman al-Zawahiri, "Ya Ahla Tunis Unsuru Shari'atakum," June 2012, CTC Library.

solution" platform to oust the dictator to championing the "battle of the *mushaf*/Qur'an," i.e., the battle to apply God's Law, reminding Muslims of the words of the founder of the Muslim Brotherhood, Hasan al-Banna, that "Islam is religion and state" (*Missive 6*). Of course this is not intended as an endorsement of the Muslim Brotherhood (MB), the politics of which he has extensively criticized,[112] but rather to highlight the extent to which the MB has departed from the teachings of its founder.

Al-Zawahiri highlighted his disdain of the MB by addressing several pointed questions to Muhammad Mursi, a few months after Mursi was elected President. A number of the questions he posed concern Mursi's position with respect to laws that contradict the Shari'a in Egypt's constitution, and whether he would uphold the peace treaty with Israel (*Missive 11*). When Mursi was ousted, al-Zawahiri shrewdly reached out to those "who are sincere and honorable and desire the victory of Islam, calling on them to unite under the banner of *tawhid*."[113] He was no doubt hoping to capitalize on the sense of disenfranchisement among MB members following Mursi's removal, but by no means was he sympathizing with the platform of the MB. Indeed, even though he explicitly stated that "I am not rejoicing at your misfortune (*shamata*)," Schadenfreude characterizes his tone when he remarks:

> What would you have lost, had you, at the start of the revolution, brought
>
> together all those working to support Islam on the basis of governing according
>
> to the Shari'a? …. Nothing. You would have [at least] gained God's blessing
>
> and [prided yourselves] on your steadfast commitment to the Islamic creed.
>
> [Had you done so] what were they going to do with you? Were they going to
>
> prohibit you from governing? They deposed you …. Were they going to arrest
>
> you? They are arresting you …. Were you going to lose the support of the world
>
> community? They are all united against you…[114]

---

[112] Ayman al-Zawahiri, *al-Hisad hasad?al-Murr: al-Ikhwan al-Muslimun fi Sittina 'Aman, Minbar al-Tawhid wa-al-Jihad*, http://www.tawhed.ws/r?i=2gxseb4t (last accessed 28 May 2013).
[113] Ayman al-Zawahiri, "Sanam al-'Ajwa al-Dimocratiyya," *Shabakat al-Fida'*, August 2013.
[114] *Ibid.*

That the MB finds itself in a predicament does not mean that al-Zawahiri is persuasive and coherent. Indeed, it is ironic that when several members of the jihadi website *Shabakat Shumukh al-Islam* took the initiative in distributing al-Zawahiri's statement to MB protesters in Rabi'a al-'Adawiyya, they were met with suspicion by some who thought that they were working for the Egyptian intelligence agency.[115] Despite highlighting the ideological dilemma facing the MB, particularly whether it should remain committed to the democratic process, the Arab Spring is forcing al-Zawahiri to confront an intractable ideological hurdle of his own. Regardless of the many setbacks the Arab Spring is experiencing, it is nevertheless clear that people harbor a strong desire to participate in elections and do not consider their participation to be in violation of their religious commitment to Islam.

Al-Zawahiri is not oblivious to this. In one statement he remarks that jihadis do not object to the principle that the umma, by which he means the Muslim people, should elect its leaders. How should people elect their leaders if elections are in violation of God's Law? Al-Zawahiri claims that electing leaders is in line with Islamic teachings. It was through the "consensus of the umma" (*ijma' al-umma*), he explains, that the first two Rightly-Guided Caliphs were appointed, and through the "choice of the people" (*ikhtiyar jumhur al-umma*) that the other two were appointed.[116] It is not unusual for religious ideologues to introduce political modernism through the back door, as al-Zawahiri is attempting to do, but he faces the difficulty of providing a framework whereby people could elect their leaders without elections.

Can al-Zawahiri go to battle with the people in support of "the battle of the *mushaf*"? Such a battle has a compelling political resonance when it's understood as an alternative to dictatorship. Now that dictators have fallen in at least three Arab countries without the help of the jihadis, al-Zawahiri is having to rely mainly on theological arguments in support of *tawhid*,[117] when, not long ago, the situation in the Middle East made a political case for him. To

---

[115] "Raddat fi'l al-Ikhwan ba'da Tawzi' al-Ikhwa Bayan al-Doctor Ayman," *Shabakat Shumukh al-Islam*, https://shamikh1.info/vb/showthread.php?t=208953 (last accessed 9 August 2013).

[116] Ayman al-Zawahiri, "Sitat wa-Arba'un 'Aman 'ala 'Am al-Naksa," Shabakat Shumukh al-Islam, https://shamikh1.info/vb/showthread.php?t=208319 (last accessed 2 August 2013).

[117] See for example Ayman al-Zawahiri, "Shamsu al-Nasri al-Bazigha 'ala al-Ummati al-Muntasira wa-al-Salibiyya al-Munhadira," September 2012, CTC Library.

his credit, he did release a short essay in November 2012, "Wathiqat Nusrat al-Islam" (charter in support of Islam), in which he succinctly outlined a political vision of *tawhid*. In it, he reiterated basic principles of jihadism, calling for the liberation of all Muslim lands, rejecting the world order of nation-states, and denouncing international law and the United Nations.[118] But if the jihadi vision did not bring down dictators in the past, the people might wonder, why should it help in a post-dictatorship world? It is unlikely that al-Zawahiri will recognize that his narrative is battling against the current, and instead that his discourse is criticizing the people whose support he is seeking.

Adam Gadahn and Husam 'Abd al-Ra'uf

Adam Gadahn and Husam 'Abd al-Ra'uf are not in the same league of global leadership as the previous four. Nevertheless, they are not affiliated with a regional jihadi group, and like the other four, their statements address the *umma* in general. Also importantly, in view of the fact that of the previous four, only al-Zawahiri remains alive, it would not be impossible for Gadahn or 'Abd al-Ra'uf to succeed al-Zawahiri. Thus far Gadahn and 'Abd al-Ra'uf have not offered any innovative approach to the Arab Spring that others have not previously considered.

The declassified documents captured in Bin Ladin's Abbottabad compound show that Gadahn was trusted and his views were respected by the senior leadership of al-Qa'ida.[119] His long letter to the senior leadership of al-Qa'ida reveals a sharp intellect and the ability to be critical not just of the West but also of various jihadi groups.[120] Yet Gadahn's reflections in response to the Arab Spring have thus far been pedestrian at best. He contends that the dictators did not fall through peaceful protest, arguing that reported violent incidents proved that the ballot box and the political process are futile. It is as if he believes that the protests that swept the MENA region are of the same order as jihad. More so than other leaders, he asserts that global jihad, particularly the 9/11 attacks, should be credited with paving the way to the revolutions in the MENA region.[121] Gadahn goes so far as to posit that "just as the jihadis made use of the internet

---

[118] Ayman al-Zawahiri, "Wathiqatu Nusrati al-Islami" November 2012, CTC Library.
[119] Brian Dodwell, "The Abbottabad Documents: The Quiet Ascent of Adam Gadahn," *CTC Sentinel*, 22 May 2012.
[120] SOCOM-2012-0000004.
[121] Adam Gadahn, "Ummat al-Tadhiya wa-al-Istishhad fi Muwajahat al-'Amala wa-al-Istibdad," Part 1.

to educate the umma and call for jihad … it is not inconceivable that the new youth opposition groups have benefited from the experience of the jihadis in their call for people to rebel against the corrupt regimes."[122] For a critical reader, it is ironic that this contention would come from Gadahn: in his Abbottabad letter he expresses his disgust at the poor quality of jihadi forums, describing them as "repulsive to most Muslims," given the religious fanaticism that most participants display.[123]

Overall, Gadahn's responses are characterized by a penchant for excessive anti-Americanism and anti-Western sentiment, even for a jihadi leader. This is demonstrably clear in his response concerning the revolution in Libya when he states: "My honorable brothers in Libya, the people of my [American] nation do not wish well by you."[124] The ironical and conflicted circumstances informing his American origin may contribute to this sanctimonious tone, but in general it is not typical of his writings. It is doubtful that he is assuming this attitude to prove his anti-American credentials to fellow jihadis, but rather to send a message to the new Arab rebels who are influenced by the West that *I know too well the traps of the West: that is why I abandoned my Western roots to join your noble umma.*

Beyond his excessive anti-Americanism, Gadahn seems to be rushing to release some of his statements that could benefit from his own critical pen. For example, Gadahn released a rather sloppy statement after the United States mounted an operation inside Libya to arrest Abu Anas al-Libi on the basis that he is an al-Qa'ida member who had participated in the 1998 East Africa embassy bombings. On the one hand, an astute jihadi audience would appreciate Gadahn's criticism of the operation, which he described as a "desperate" and "cowardly" attempt by Obama to cover up his reneging on his threat to launch a military campaign against the Syrian regime in response to the August 2013 massacre in Ghouta that was reported to have involved

---

[122] *Ibid.*
[123] SOCOM-2012-0000004, p. 4.
[124] Adam Gadahn, "Ummat al-Tadhiya wa-al-Istishhad fi Muwajahat al-'Amala wa-al-Istibdad," Part 4.

the use of chemical weapons.[125] On the other hand, the same jihadi audience would not approve of Gadahn's guidance of how the Muslims of Libya should respond to Abu Anas' arrest: while it is true that he encourages them "to teach" the United States "that the world of Islam is a red line," he undermines his own jihadi stance when he calls on Libyans not to settle "for anything less than to cut all relations with and suspend all ties to America until the safe return of Abi Anas to his people and family."[126] If Gadahn reflected on his statement before releasing it, he would have omitted this last line altogether, for surely he does not intend to suggest that if Abu Anas is freed, the Libyans could resume diplomatic ties with the United States!

In June 2013, a certain Husam 'Abd al-Ra'uf has surfaced in jihadi media, releasing an audio statement entitled "Risala li-al-Umma" (Missive to the Umma). Al-Ra'uf is not new to the jihadi scene. According to the biographical profile supplied with his statement, he was born in Egypt in 1958, and in 1989 he traveled to Pakistan where he worked for six years in Maktab al-Khadamat, which was founded by the pioneering jihadi ideologue 'Abdallah 'Azzam.[127] In 1995 he moved to Kabul to oversee charitable work, including managing several orphanages. Since 2005 he has served as the editor-in-chief of the magazine Tala'i' Khurasan.[128] It is worth noting that his short bio does not mention affiliation with al-Qa'ida. Although he has authored several short essays in response to the Arab Spring, his sudden appearance in an audio public statement produced by al-Sahab and published by al-Fajr, the media outlets of al-Qa'ida, significantly alters assessments of his vocation. If he continues to release such statements, it is possible that he is being promoted as a candidate who might succeed al-Zawahiri.

It is noteworthy that his first audio statement is focused on rejecting the charges that the Arab Spring has undermined jihadism. As with other leaders, 'Abd al-Ra'uf struggles between embracing the revolutions and arguing that jihadis aspire towards different goals. For example,

---

[125] Adam Gadahn, "Jarimatu Ikhtitafi Abi Anas al-Libi," *Shabakat Shumukh al-Islam*, statement released in November 2013 and posted on al-Shumukh on 1 December 2013, https://shamikh1.info/vb/showthread.php?t=215529 (accessed 2 December 2013).

[126] *Ibid.*

[127] On 'Azzam's critical role in mobilizing Muslims to fight in Afghanistan, see Thomas Hegghammer, "The Origins of Global Jihad: Explaining the Arab Mobilization to 1980s Afghanistan," (Policy Memo, International Security Program, Belfer Center for Science and International Affairs, Harvard Kennedy School, 22 January 2009). Hegghammer is completing a book concerning 'Azzam.

[128] Husam 'Abd al-Ra'uf, "Risala li-al-Umma," June 2013, CTC Library.

on the one hand, he remarks that all jihadi groups "supported the revolutions and … our [jihadi] leaders who were released from prisons and detention centers are serving in the battlefields, they are guiding the public."[129] On the other hand, he is keen to distinguish al-Qa'ida's objectives from those of the revolutions, stating that al-Qa'ida "does not pursue political change for the sake of change … rather it seeks a radical and genuine change."[130] As far as he is concerned, the current outcome of the revolutions that brought down the rulers in Tunisia, Egypt, Libya and Yemen is not "what was hoped for."

What 'Abd al-Ra'uf envisages for these countries is an Islamic state such as that which he experienced under the Taliban. Short of that, he swears an oath that the umma shall not enjoy security except under Shari'a. It is not clear if this oath is a threat or that he is simply calling on people to apply the Shari'a. At any rate, 'Abd al-Ra'uf evinces very little respect for the masses. "The people," he holds, "continue to be driven by their natural instinct and they merely need someone in whom they can trust so that he may guide them and lead them to their happiness in this world and the next."[131] He holds the American public in similar contempt. In an article entitled "The Revolution of the American Spring" published soon after the Occupy Wall Street movement began, 'Abd al-Ra'uf attributes the protests to the economic hardship he believes plagues the Western world as a result of poor and corrupt leadership. Yet instead of using compelling political arguments, as Bin Ladin did in his addresses to the American public,[132] 'Abd al-Ra'uf settled for a vulgar slur, addressing them as "O stupid American public."[133] If 'Abd al-Ra'uf is indeed being promoted as a global jihadi leader, he is recasting the role with a substantially altered tone: it is an approach that succeeds in editorials published in Tala'i' Khurasan, but it is arguably misplaced in audio statements that demean those whose support he is seeking.

---

[129] *Ibid.*

[130] *Ibid.*

[131] *Ibid.*

[132] See for example Usama b. Ladin, 'The Towers of Lebanon,' in Bruce Lawrence (ed.), *Messages to the World: The Statements of Osama bin Laden* (trans. by James Howarth), London/New York: Verso, 2005, p. 238.

[133] Husam 'Abd al-Ra'uf, "Thawratu al-Rabi'i al-Amrikiyya," 5 October 2011, *Shabakat al-Fida' al-Islamiyya,* http://alfidaa.org/vb/showthread.php?t=13260 (last accessed 2 October 2013).

Concluding Remarks

"To whom does Judgment belong? To the people or their Creator?" asks Ayman al-Zawahiri in one of his statements. "If sovereignty lies with the people," he adds, "then we lost before we even entered into the battle" (*Missive 9*). The majority of the people in Tunisia, Egypt and Libya responded in a wholly other way to this question: their rush to cast their votes is a statement that is *buwah*, clear.

Has the Arab Spring weakened jihadi discourse? To the distant observer, the fractious political situation in Tunisia, Egypt and Libya may not currently inspire much confidence in the stability of the region. But a close reading of statements by jihadi leaders in response to the Arab Spring reveals that beneath gloating triumphalist rhetoric lies despair as to what jihadi identity and ideology represent. Their despair is rooted in two main causes. At a fundamental level, with the fall of dictators the jihadi narrative lost its soul. Now that the jihadi grievance lies prevailingly with the people, the jihadi narrative begins to lose the credibility it once enjoyed. While it may be virtuous to condemn a dictator, it is dangerous to mock the people, even if the people appear to be engaged in establishing an idiocracy.

On a related level, jihadism is now suffering from convoluted, often fallacious rationalizations in an attempt to defend the relevance of its ideals. The post-9/11 decade was the decade of jihadism, when jihadi leaders were perceived as significant to the political and national structure of society worldwide. Accordingly, the attention of the world was on the "few" who spoke on behalf of the "many" they did not in good faith represent. The Arab Spring, by contrast – and until the conflict in Syria turned bloody – focused global attention on the "many" for whom jihadism is irrelevant in their *tahrir* enterprise.

Chapter Two   Arab Spring Jihadism: Jihadis without Jihad?

Within months of the onset of the Arab Spring, countries that underwent regime change witnessed the emergence of new groups that embrace and project a jihadi worldview, with many of them featuring the "Ansar al-Shari'a" motif in their names. The emergence of these groups generates several pertinent questions: has the Arab Spring provided fertile ground for jihadi ideology? Who are the new jihadi groups that have emerged since the onset of the Arab Spring and which have positioned themselves as interlocutors in global jihadi discourse? And what kind of influence are they likely to have on the political course of countries that underwent regime change since the Arab Spring? This chapter argues that rapid growth in the number of these groups does not necessarily reflect the strength of traditional jihadism characterized by active militancy. Rather than acting upon principles of jihad, these groups appear instead to be more interested in its rhetoric.

This chapter presents a panoramic view of the new jihadi landscape that has emerged in countries that have undergone regime change as a result of the Arab Spring, namely Tunisia, Egypt and Libya. It consists of two broad sections: the first identifies the inconsistency of the new jihadi groups from the perspective of traditional jihadism and the way in which they differ. It also highlights why this inconsistency presents a challenge to define or categorize these new groups from a scholarly perspective. The second section analyzes the founding statements of many of the new jihadi groups; it evaluates their operational credentials vis-à-vis their rhetorical intentions; and it also explores the extent to which their discourse is in keeping with the norms advocated by the broader global jihadi discourse.

Traditional Jihadism and New Jihadi Groups

Ideological Inconsistency: the Deed of Inaction

Within months of the onset of the Arab Spring, countries that underwent regime change witnessed the emergence of new groups that embrace and project a jihadi worldview. For the purpose of this report, the study focuses on new groups that have emerged only in countries that underwent regime change as a result of the Arab Spring, namely Tunisia, Egypt and Libya. It does not examine Yemen: the transfer of power from President 'Abdallah Saleh to his Vice President 'Abd Rabbuh Mansour Hadi does not constitute regime change in the same way or to the extent that Tunisia, Egypt and Libya experienced change; Hadi was elected President in February 2012 in an election in which he was the only candidate. As at the time of writing this report, Syria also has not undergone a regime change, but since the war has been a magnet for many local and foreign fighters, its effects on jihadism will be discussed in the concluding chapter of this report.

Many of the new jihadi groups that have emerged in Tunisia, Egypt and Libya feature the "Ansar al-Shari'a" motif in their names. Literally, the name designates those who regard themselves as supporters or partisans of the application of God's Law in the public and private spheres. As a general designation, all devout Muslims could qualify as *ansar al-shari'a* in the private sphere; but most of them, as the Arab Spring has shown, do not believe that partaking in the secular political processes that govern their public sphere violate their commitment to the Islamic faith. In the case of new jihadi groups, however, the name Ansar al-Shari'a is purposely used to express their opposition to the new regimes and the laws that govern the state. In their minds, the people's revolutions brought down the tyrant, but the unjust and oppressive man-made laws (i.e., *al-qawanin al-wad 'iyya*, "positive law") are still in place and Muslims therefore remain subject to tyrannical rule. As such, new jihadi groups are committed to replacing positive law with God's Law in order to ensure that divine justice reigns for all.

As noted in the introduction, these new groups are yet to develop a consistent ideological framework that brings consonance between their rhetoric and their action. The jihadi legal scholar Abu Mundhir al-Shanqiti wrote a short essay in which he developed a broad framework that he believes is encompassed by the name "Ansar al-Shari'a," and it is essentially designed to create an alternative political platform to that proffered by the secular movers of the Arab Spring. From his perspective, the name is of sublime value that cannot be matched by the secular values that others espouse. In his words, "since there are those who associate their names with terms such as 'justice,' 'freedom,' 'development,' 'reform' and 'light' … we shall associate our name with al-Shari'a."[134] In addition, he also wants to distinguish among conservative religious Muslims lest they all be perceived to be the same. In particular, he is keen to distinguish "Ansar al-Shari'a" from "Salafis," since many Salafis have formed political parties and contested elections in the wake of the Arab Spring, thereby embracing positive law while still projecting an aura of strict adherence to Islamic Law.[135] It should be noted that al-Shanqiti does not speak on behalf of all new groups, and not all of them are called "Ansar al-Shari'a;" some of them are happy to use the name "Salafi-Jihadis" in the same spirit as that conveyed by al-Shanqiti.

Yet despite the new groups' opposition not just to the regimes but also to the very nature of what constitutes legitimacy, and despite their threatening militant rhetoric, they have largely refrained from translating their jihadism into action. Viewed in the context of what traditional jihadism stands for, the pertinence of this emerging trend of jihadiless jihadis cannot be overstated. Indeed, traditional jihadism conceives of jihad as the essential path towards bringing about a genuine Islamic society. Until such a society exists, jihad and religious concepts such as *tawhid* or Shari'a are deemed by jihadis to be two sides of the same coin. While it is true that traditional jihadi groups do not all agree on strategy, ideology and tactics when it comes to implementing jihad, nevertheless they all share a commitment to the deed of jihad and are prepared to make enormous sacrifices to advance the jihadi project.

By contrast, new jihadi groups appear to be hesitant jihadis at most. They have rapidly established media outlets through which their official statements are released. They are also taking advantage of the new freedoms brought about by the Arab Spring to promote their worldview publicly: they uphold the principle of the obligation of jihad, advance anti-democratic rhetoric using religious arguments, and lionize global jihadi leaders and their causes. Yet, for now, their operational credentials are scarce, they are characterized more readily by the propaganda of jihad than by its delivery.

---

[134] Abu al-Mundhir al-Shanqiti, "Nahnu Ansar al-Shari'a," *Minbar al-Tawhid wa-al-Jihad*, 29 May 2012, http://www.tawhed.ws/a?a=shanqeet (last accessed 29 May 2013).
[135] *Ibid.*

This is not to suggest or predict that new jihadi groups will not carry out violent operations in the future. Rather, it is to observe that given their adamant ideological opposition to the new regimes combined with their staunch militant rhetoric and commitment to the obligation of jihad to implement God's Law, one would have expected these new groups to avail themselves of recent opportunities to engage in violent operations during the period of political transition in Tunisia, Egypt and Libya.

As will be discussed in the section below, new jihadi groups call on their supporters to join jihad in Syria – and occasionally in Mali – and while they deny the legitimacy of their home regimes, they do not seem willing to rebel against them. This presents a quandary: if they are convinced, as they assert, that the regimes in Tunisia, Egypt and Libya are in clear violation of God's Law, why should they believe that the path to paradise passes through Syria? Despite their solidarity with Ayman al-Zawahiri, they seem to have forgotten that when he was living as a jihadi in Egypt, he maintained through words and deeds that "the road to Jerusalem passes through Cairo," by which he meant that jihad against the regime in Cairo was deserving of the jihadis' attention before that of Israel.[136] It is true, as indicated in the previous chapter, that al-Zawahiri himself is now struggling to provide a coherent jihadi path. In this respect, these new jihadi groups are no longer part of the traditional jihadi fold and exhibit a preference to remain as conversational, and not operational, partners with global jihadi groups.

What has changed?

In his seminal work "The Four Waves of Terrorism," the great scholar of terrorism David Rapoport remarked that one of the reasons terrorist waves come to an end is due to "a human life cycle pattern, where dreams that inspire fathers lose their attractiveness for the sons."[137] This would have been an appealing theory that might explain traditional jihadism's commitment to deeds and new jihadi groups' commitment to rhetoric instead. However, in most cases we are not dealing with the generational change of fathers and sons, but rather with fathers who were

---

[136] Ayman al-Zawahiri, "al-Tariq ila al-Quds Yamurru 'Abra al-Qahira," *Minbar al-Tawhid wa-al-Jihad*, http://www.tawhed.ws/r?i=4wwr6wa8 (last accessed 17 May 2013).
[137] David Rapoport, "The Four Waves of Terrorism," *Current History*, December 2001, pp. 419-25.

once traditional active jihadis and are now part of the new wave of new ostensibly passive jihadis.

The lack of operational activities on the part of new jihadi groups does not escape active jihadis. Abu Jalal al-Shami, a member of the legal committee of Majlis Shura al-Mujahidin, wrote a short treatise commenting on the meaning of two Qur'anic verses that speak about God's anger with those whose deeds do not correspond with their words: "O true believers, why do ye say that which ye do not? It is most odious in the sight of GOD, that ye say that which ye do not." (Q. 61: 2-3 – Sales translation). Abu Bilal draws on this verse to highlight its relevance for today and to chastise those whom he believes are in dire need of reflecting on this verse and applying it to their lives: "the true believer," he explains, "and the sincere jihadi does not allow his deed to be inconsistent with his word … today, we are in need of inviting people to join us in our mission by way of [displaying] our disciplined and actual action before we invite them with our word." Abu Bilal's treatise is not addressing only those whom he considers to be nominal Muslims in power, such as the Muslim Brotherhood (MB); rather, his treatise is addressed to those who are part of the "global jihadi mission" (da'wat al-jihad al-'alami) and the Salafi-Jihadi mission (al-da'wa al-salafiyya al-mujahida), specifically cited in his writings in red ink.[138] If Abu Bilal's worry is justified, then passive jihadis may constitute a developing trend that is of concern to active jihadis.

One may of course argue that the new jihadi groups are not passive, that they are instead at a stage of preparation (i'dad), and as they consolidate they will eventually instigate their own Jihad Spring. While this is possible, it is also the case that with time people may well grow used to understanding jihadism as a rhetorical formulation that does not involve action, other than demonstrations and the raising of black flags. Over time, such an understanding of jihad may, unwittingly, help the cause of mainstream Muslims who stress that jihad is only a spiritual and internal struggle. If this is a plausible forecast, new jihadi groups risk turning jihadism into an "ism," akin to that of Pan-Arabism. Those versed in Pan-Arabist discourse know too well that

---

[138] Abu Bilal al-Shami, *Ta'ammulat Nazir al-Taraf fi Ayat min Surat al-Saff*, Shabakat Ansar al-Mujahidin, posted on 19 May 2013, http://www.bbc.co.uk/arabic/middleeast/2013/04/130429_libya_latest.shtml (last accessed 20 May 2013).

the rhetoric of Pan-Arabism used to be repeatedly vocalized by virtually every Arab leader, but it mostly materialized in the emotional poems composed by leading Arab poets and sung by divas to crowds of the faithful, some of whom continue to await the Pan-Arabist rapture.

What then is the political identity of these new groups and what kind of influence might they have?

The path the new groups are pursuing makes their political identity difficult to define: they cannot be said to be jihadis in the traditional sense, because jihadis have proven themselves not through the deed of propaganda but by the "propaganda of the deed," to borrow Carlo Pisacane's famous phrase. They cannot be said to fit the description of what scholars refer to as a "social movement," in that they are not excluded from the establishment and are seeking to be recognized by it as a legitimate entity.[139] Put differently, they are not disenfranchised, and they reject being enfranchised on the basis of voting and citizenship. Instead, they want to transform the nature of the establishment, but without resorting to revolutionary violence. Furthermore, they cannot be said to fit the description of what scholars define as "civil society" actors since they are not, in principle, content with coexisting with other components of civil society or with the government.[140]

It is perhaps unreasonable to expect that new jihadi groups should have already developed a program of action that corresponds to an internally coherent ideology. But given that they defy a typology, it is reasonable to ponder the extent to which they can continue to project but not implement a jihadi worldview and maintain an uncompromising stance vis-à-vis the political process. In principle there is no reason why such groups could not sustain rhetoric and inaction, but one would expect them to shrink in size and remain outliers, similar to the anti-Zionist

---

[139] I am going by the understanding of social movements as described by Charles Tilly, *Contentious Performances*, New York: Columbia University Press, 2008, p. 121.

[140] For a number of inclusive definitions of civil society, see Larry Diamond, "Rethinking Civil Society: Toward Democratic Consolidation," *Journal of Democracy*, 5 (1994): 4–18, p. 5; John Keane, "Civil Society, Definitions and Approaches" (entry in the Encyclopedia of Civil Society, Springer) at http://www.johnkeane.net/pdf_docs/civil_society/jk_civil_sciety_definitions_encyclopedia.pdf , 7 January 2010; Philippe Schmitter, "Civil Society East and West," in Larry Diamond, Marc F. Plattner, Yun-han Chu, and Hung-mao Tien, eds., *Consolidating the Third Wave Democracies: Themes and Perspectives*, Baltimore: Johns Hopkins University Press, 1997, p. 240.

Jewish group Neturei Karta in Israel.[141] Since they object to voting, they are unlikely to influence the agenda of Islamist or other groups contesting elections.

However, the jihadi worldview of these new groups could be translated into action for reasons that are not accounted for by the leadership of these groups. To begin with, it is perhaps a blessing for these passive jihadi leaders that there is a "jihad" waging in Syria, and less so in Mali, in which Tunisians, Libyans and Egyptians can serve as full-time jihadis. Indeed, the situation in Syria seems to occasion joint statements by leaders of different groups, providing them with a rallying cause. The fact that the leader of the Lebanon-based Shi'ite group Hizbullah – Hasan Nasrallah – has explicitly promised victory in Syria, making it clear that his group is involved in combat in Syria,[142] has also given new jihadi groups a sectarian mission, calling on their supporters to target countries that are predominantly governed by "al-Rafida," which is the pejorative term used by sectarian Sunnis to designate Shi'ites.[143] But in the event that those who volunteer to fight in Syria return home if the situation there stabilizes, these active jihadis may be less inclined to remain passive upon their return, a scenario akin to that of returnees from Afghanistan in Algeria and elsewhere. It is also possible that active jihadism may be unleashed not by the design of the leaders, but through the actions of frustrated members or former members,[144] or those inspired by their rhetoric. There is no reason why the phenomenon of jihadi self-radicalization – for instance the examples of Major Nidal Hasan in the United States,[145] or Roshonara Choudhry in Britain[146] – would not take place in Muslim-

---

[141] For a description of religious political parties in Israel, see Gershon Shafir and Yoav Peled, *Being Israeli: The Dynamics of Multiple Citizenship*, Cambridge: Cambridge University Press, 2002, pp. 110-55.

[142] See the transcript of Hasan Nasrallah's speech, "Kama Kuntu A'idukum bi-al-Nasri Da'iman A'idukum bi-al-Nasri Mujaddadan," *Qanat al-Manar*, 25 May 2013, http://www.almanar.com.lb/adetails.php?eid=498289&frid=21&seccatid=19&cid=21&fromval=1 (last accessed 28 May 2013).

[143] See the joint statement signed by, among others, Muhammad al-Zawahiri, Jalal Abu al-Futuh, Sayyid Abu Khadra, "Nasra li-Ahlina fi al-Qusayr," *Shabakat Shumukh al-Islam*, 26 May 2013, https://shamikh1.info/vb/showthread.php?t=202175 (last accessed 28 May 2013).

[144] One such example is Bryant Neal Vinus, who is believed to have been dissatisfied with the Islamic Thinkers Society as mere "talkers," Paul Cruickshank, Nic Robertson and Ken Shiffman, "The Radicalization of an All American Kid," *CNN*, 15 May 2010, http://www.cnn.com/2010/CRIME/05/13/bryant.neal.vinas.part1/index.html (last accessed 30 May 2013). My thanks to Brian Dodwell for drawing this example to my attention.

[145] Scott Shane and James Dao, "Investigators Study Tangle of Clues on Fort Hood Suspect," *The New York Times*, 14 November 2009, http://www.nytimes.com/2009/11/15/us/15hasan.html?pagewanted=all&_r=0 (last accessed 29 May 2013). See also email correspondence between Hasan and al-'Awalaki posted on Intelwire, 19 July 2012, http://news.intelwire.com/2012/07/the-following-e-mails-between-maj.html (last accessed 29 May 2013).

majority countries. In either case, we would perhaps witness some of the leaders being silently co-opted by the establishment to avoid prison sentences; a similar predicament facing some Saudi religious scholars when the government repressed jihadi activities in the Kingdom.[147] They may even be enlisted to rehabilitate those who deviate from what is considered to be the proper understanding of jihad.

To illustrate the ideological inconsistencies mentioned above, in the section that follows new jihadi groups are divided according to the countries where they are based. Their ideological worldview is assessed based on categorization of their public releases and the context of their media communications and operational credentials. Given that jihadi websites are used as the main primary source upon which the analysis is based, it is difficult to ascertain the extent of support these groups enjoy. The list of the new groups provided does not claim to be an exhaustive one.

TUNISIA

Tunisia is the birthplace of the Arab Spring: in December 2010 the young vendor Muhammad Bouazizi, whose fruit and vegetable cart was arbitrarily confiscated by the police, set himself on fire outside his local municipal office. The group Ansar al-Shari'a emerged in Tunisia within months of the revolution. One of the group's vocal leaders, Abu 'Iyad al-Tunisi, a *kunya* for Sayf Allah b. Hussein, stresses that the Tunisian Ansar al-Shari'a predates the group by the same name in Yemen. So keen is he to emphasize this fact that if doubters "wanted to be sure, [they should] look up the date of the first gathering or conference Ansar al-Shari'a organized in May 2011 that took place in the suburb of al-Sukara, following which, within four or five days, the organization Ansar al-Shari'a in Yemen announced its formation."[148] Abu 'Iyad is of course not claiming copyright for the name Ansar al-Shari'a, but given that the name has become

---

[146] "Roshonara Choudhry: Police interview extracts," *The Guardian*, November 3, 2010, http://www.guardian.co.uk/uk/2010/nov/03/roshonara-choudhry-police-interview.

[147] Thomas Hegghammer, *Jihad in Saudi Arabia: Violence and Pan-Islamism since 1979*, Cambridge: Cambridge University Press, 2010, p. 154-60. For additional background on state repression of religious scholars, see Stéphane Lacroix, *Awakening Islam: The Politics of Religious Dissent in Contemporary Saudi Arabia*, Cambridge, MA: Harvard University Press, 2011, pp. 202-25.

[148] Interview with Abu 'Iyad al-Tunisi, *al-Shumukh*, 14 February 2013, https://shamikh1.info/vb/showthread.php?t=191646&highlight=%DA%ED%C7%D6 (last accessed 7 May 2013).

representative of a new wave that has emerged since the Arab Spring and which claims to be uncorrupted by positive law,[149] he would like his group to be credited with having pioneered this development.

Abu 'Iyad's Facebook page introduces him as a "shrewd 45-year old politician with years of jihad experience," and proudly notes that "he kept the company of Abu Qatada" – the Palestinian jihadi ideologue who was until recently based in the United Kingdom,[150] adding that Abu 'Iyad "was part of the jihad in Afghanistan … and for years he was blacklisted by many governments until he was arrested in Turkey then handed to the Tunisian government which falsely sentenced him to 43 years in prison." [151] Following the fall of the regime Abu 'Iyad was released from prison in March 2011, eight years into his sentence.[152] He is credited with having participated in the founding of a group called *al-Jama'a al-Tunisiyya al-Muqatila fi Afghanistan* (The Tunisian Combatant Group in Afghanistan – TCG),[153] before he became leader of a militant group called *Saraya al-Da'wa wa-al-Jihad* (Missionary Activities and Jihad [Military] Company) in 2000. TCG is said to have been involved in the assassination of Ahmed Shah Mas'ud, the leader of the Northern Alliance in Afghanistan in 2001.[154] Usama b. Ladin – and al-Qa'ida – is often

---

[149] For a discussion of various religious groups with a violent agenda, see Anne Wolf, "Tunisia: Signs of Domestic Radicalization Post-Revolution," *CTC Sentinel*, January 2013, vol. 6, Issue, pp. 1-4. See also Anne Wolf and Raphael Lefevre "The demon or the demonized? Deconstructing 'Salafism' in Tunisia," OpenDemocracy, 5 June 2012, http://www.opendemocracy.net/print/66234 (last accessed 1 April 2013).

[150] For years, Abu Qatada was based in the UK fighting a legal battle against extradition to Jordan; he was extradited to Jordon in July 2013, see "Mahkamat Amn al-Dawla bi-al-Urdun Ta-tasallam Abu Qatada," *Al-Jazeera*, 7 July 2013, http://www.aljazeera.net/news/pages/caeec1b2-148f-4279-8e7b-af6d0d9093e0 (linked accessed on the same day).

[151] Abu 'Iyad al-Tunisi, *Facebook*, http://www.facebook.com/pages/%D8%A7%D9%84%D8%B4%D9%8A%D8%AE-%D8%A3%D8%A8%D9%88-%D8%B9%D9%8A%D8%A7%D8%B6-%D8%A7%D9%84%D8%AA%D9%88%D9%86%D8%B3%D9%8A/101548453257941?id=101548453257941&sk=info (last accessed 29 March 2013).

[152] *Ibid*.

[153] For background information about the group, see "Security Council Committee pursuant to resolutions 1267 (1999) and 1989 (2011) concerning al-Qaida and associated individual entities', *United Nations*, http://www.un.org/sc/committees/1267/NSQE09002E.shtml. The UN narrative summary regarding this group notes that it was listed on "10 October 2002 pursuant to paragraphs 1 and 2 of resolution 1390 (2002)" as being associated with Al-Qaida, Usama bin Laden or the Taliban for "participating in the financing, planning, facilitating, preparing or perpetrating of acts or activities by, in conjunction with, under the name of, on behalf or in support of" and "recruiting for" Usama bin Laden, Al-Qaida (QE.A.4.01) and the Organization of Al-Qaida in the Islamic Maghreb."

[154] Muhammad Abu Rumman and Hasan Abu Haniyyi, "'Ansar al-Shari'a': Ashkal Istijabat 'al-Qa'ida' li-al-Tahawwul al-Dimucrati fi al-'Alam al-'Arabi," *al-Hayat*, 3 May 2013, http://alhayat.com/Details/468532 (last accessed 13 May 2013).

reported as being responsible for the assassination;[155] if both claims are true, it would suggest that TCG and al-Qa'ida collaborated at least in 2001.

The apparatus of the Tunisian Ansar al-Shari'a, as explained on its website, consists of a legal committee and four different bureaux: political; media; missionary; and social welfare bureaux; with the legal committee providing guidance on whether the group's statements and activities conform to Islamic legal codes of conduct. The group's activities are promoted through the group's website,[156] an online forum,[157] a Facebook page,[158] and the magazine *Promise* (*Majallat al-Wa'd*).[159] The group also maintains its own media arm, Mu'assasat al-Bayariq al-I'lamiyya: it publishes the group's public statements and audio-visual releases on major jihadi forums such as *Shabakat Ansar al-Mujahidin, Shabakat al-Fida' al-Islamiyya* and *Shabakat Shumukh al-Islam*.[160] The website includes an announcement promising to launch a radio station on the internet.

The mission statement of Ansar al-Shari'a echoes the rigid religious worldview of the jihadi ideologue Abu Muhammad al-Maqdisi,[161] whose website it promotes; it calls for "forsaking [worldly pleasures and devoting oneself exclusively to] God (*al-hijra ila Allah*) through professing a passion for divine unity (*tawhid*) and dissociating from [all forms of] idolatry (*shirk*)

---

[155] John Tagliabue with Susan Sachs, "A Nation Challenged: A Tangled Web," *The New York Times*, 8 December 2001, http://www.nytimes.com/2001/12/08/world/nation-challenged-tangled-web-european-cell-al-qaeda-cited-killing-massoud.html?ref=ahmedshahmassoud (last accessed 13 May 2013).
Paul Cruickshank, " Suicide bomber's widow soldiers on," *CNN*, 24 August 2006, http://www.cnn.com/2006/WORLD/asiapcf/08/15/elaroud/index.html (last accessed 13 May 2013).
[156] *Ansar al-Shari'a bi- Tunis, http://ansar-ashariaa.com/*
[157] *Ansar al-Shari'a bi- Tunis, http://www.ansar-alsharee3a.com/index.php*
[158] https://www.facebook.com/ansar.shari3a.touness?ref=stream
[159] It is accessed through the website of the group.
[160] *Shabakat al-Fida' al-Islamiyya* and *Shabakat Shumukh al-Islam* are accredited by Markaz al-Fajr li-al-I'lam, which is the "official" jihadi media distributor, serving as the exclusive distributor of al-Sahab production materials, as well as other media production such as al-Andalus (which produces al-Qa'ida in the Islamic Maghreb materials). See for instance the statement it released in September 2012 on *Shabakat al-Shumukh*, https://shamikh1.info/vb/showthread.php?t=176648&highlight=%C7%E1%CA%DE%E4%ED%C9. *Shabakat Ansar al-Mujahidin* is also reliable in so far as releasing official jihadi statements, but given that it does not require membership to enter the website, it is less secure from a jihadi perspective than the other two sites. It should be noted that these websites are occasionally hacked and cease to operate for periods of time.
[161] For a comprehensive view of al-Maqdisi's worldview, see Nelly Lahoud, "In Search of Philosopher-Jihadis: Abu Muhammad al-Maqdisi's Jihadi Philosophy," *Journal of Totalitarian Movements and Political Religions*, Volume 10, Issue 2, 2009, pp. 205 – 220; Joas Wagemakers, *A Quietist Jihadi: The Ideology and Influence of Abu Muhammad al-Maqdisi*, Cambridge: Cambridge University Press, 2012.

and insult [that may offend God]."[162] Like al-Maqdisi, the group holds a strong anti-democratic stance, believing democracy to be a form of religion that compromises God's divine unity. The group also promotes the writings of other jihadi ideologues as well as the news of active jihadi groups, e.g., al-Shabab in Somalia, Emirate of Kavkaz in the Caucasus region. Through its magazine, the group encourages cyberwarfare and lists an advertisement for a course that teaches hacking.[163] The group's magazine has even encouraged Tunisian youth to join the fight in Syria.[164]

Yet despite projecting a jihadi worldview, Ansar al-Shari'a and its leaders are more preoccupied with distancing themselves from jihadi activities than with proving their jihadi credentials. As far as the operational dimension of the group is concerned, Ansar al-Shari'a, notwithstanding its support for jihad elsewhere, does not call on its supporters to engage in jihad in Tunisia. In fact, it claims that it "does not intend to raise arms," adding the mandatory anti-American bluster, implying that its peaceful stance is conditional on the United States "not interfering between us and our people."[165]

At one point, the group's political bureau considered the possibility of engaging in unconditional dialogue with all parties in Tunisia "without exception," claiming that "dialogue and only dialogue is the solution." Soon thereafter, however, it withdrew this invitation upon receiving a letter from its Legal Committee. It is possible that its Legal Committee pointed out that engaging in dialogue with political parties that embraced democracy, including the ruling Islamist party Hizb al-Nahda, would violate Ansar al-Shari'a's commitment to dissociate from all forms of idolatry. To its credit, the group admitted the mistake in a transparent fashion and released a retraction indicating that its activities are devoted "to rebuilding a generation that would lift this great religion and raise the banner of *tawhid*." Such a blunder suggests a lack of understanding of the ideological and political parameters in which Ansar al-Shari'a and other

---

[162]See "Hadhihi Da'watuna," *Ansar al-Shari'a bi-Tunis*, http://ansar-ashariaa.com/index.php/2013-02-04-20-18-27 (last accessed 28 February 2013).

[163] See the first issue of the group's magazine *Majallat al-Wa'd*, p. 13.

[164] *Majallat al-Wa'd*, p. 15.

[165] *Ansar al-Shari'a bi-Tunis*, http://ansar-ashariaa.com/index.php/2013-02-16-21-33-03/2013-02-16-21-36-58/78-2013-02-26-10-24-39 (last accessed 28 February 2013).

jihadi groups operate. Just in case the group's rigid supporters feared that Ansar al-Shari'a's move towards dialogue might lead to electioneering, Abu 'Iyad later asserted that his group would never consider partaking in the "political game": "as far as we are concerned, the issue of elections is settled."[166]

But if building a generation that understands the principles of *tawhid* should be considered by jihadis as the focus in Tunisia, why shouldn't the same approach apply elsewhere? In other words, why shouldn't all jihadis suspend jihad and focus on instilling the principles of *tawhid* among the public? By the same token, if jihad is justified elsewhere, why is it not justified in Tunisia since its regime is, in Ansar al-Shari'a view, in violation of God's Law? These two alternatives, or perhaps dilemmas, highlight the glaring ideological inconsistencies of Tunisia's Ansar al-Shari'a. For a group that promotes the obligation of jihad, Ansar al-Shari'a is far from convincingly defining the role of jihad in its worldview. For example, Abu 'Iyad categorically asserts that the protest that led to the ousting of Bin 'Ali does not qualify as a revolution: "Is a revolution," he passionately asks, "merely about removing the head of state while keeping his regime in place?" Yet, in the same interview, he maintains that "jihad has its causes which are not available in Tunisia. Yes [I am talking about] jihad in the sense of raising arms, if its causes exist in Tunisia, the tens even hundreds of Tunisian youth would not be emigrating to Syria and elsewhere [to carry out jihad]."[167] The outsider, perhaps one day the insider, may well ask why an "apostate" regime such as Syria deserves to be removed through jihad while a seemingly similar "apostate" regime such as Tunisia does not deserve the same.

The ambiguity of the role of jihad in Ansar al-Shari'a's discourse has communicated mixed signals to active jihadi groups elsewhere. Some of the references in the group's literature encouraging Tunisian youth to participate in jihad in Syria understandably caught the attention of and likely displeased al-Qa'ida in the Islamic Maghreb (AQIM). From the perspective of AQIM, which seeks to turn the Maghreb region into its own domain, it could use the help of local and foreign jihadis in this endeavor. Thus AQIM is keen to make it known to the jihadi

---

[166] Abu 'Iyad al-Tunisi, interview on 30 January 2013, http://www.youtube.com/watch?v=rRfIauOG H6w&feature=youtu.be
[167] Abu 'Iyad al-Tunisi, interview on 30 January 2013.

enthusiasts in Tunisia that Syria is a long voyage they needn't make when they can perform the duty of jihad in their own backyard.

AQIM made sure that its own stakes were understood by Ansar al-Shari'a. It released a carefully crafted statement addressed to Muslim youth in the Islamic Maghreb in general and "in Tunisia in particular."[168] The bulk of the statement deals with the Islamic legal ruling on the permissibility and obligation of *hijra* (emigration) from the abode of unbelief (*dar al-kufr*) to either another abode of unbelief that is less harmful for Muslims or to an abode of Islam (*dar al-Islam*) where God's Law reigns. As with most jihadi statements, the religious legal discussion is designed to serve a specific agenda. In this case, AQIM warns Tunisian youth not to abandon Tunisia to the secularists who will corrupt it; but the heart of the message is to make it known to Tunisians that if it is deemed lawful for them to perform the *hijra*; that their surrounding region is more entitled to their services than elsewhere, no doubt implying that Syria should not be their first destination:

> He from among the Muslim youth who has been banished by the criminal and oppressive [authorities], or whomever the jihadi leadership deems that the benefits of his *hijra* outweigh his stay, we call on him to join the jihad caravan in the Islamic Maghreb where the struggle is raging and the war is aggravated against your fellow jihadi brethren due to the French Crusader campaign against Islamic northern Mali or the Algerian northern front … the Islamic Maghreb front today has utmost need for the support of the sons of Tunisia, Morocco, Libya, Mauritania to repel the onslaught of France the Crusader and to drive away its agents from the region.[169]

Some two months prior to AQIM's statement and within three weeks of France's military intervention in Mali, Abu 'Iyad had indicated that Tunisian youth should remain at home because both Syria and Mali enjoy a sufficient number of jihadis; an unusual, if not a

---

[168] AQIM, "Nida' ila Shabab al-Islam," 17 March 2013, *Shabakat Shumukh al-Islam*, https://shamikh1.info/vb/showthread.php?t=195150

[169] AQIM, "Nida' ila Shabab al-Islam," 17 March 2013, *Shabakat Shumukh al-Islam*, https://shamikh1.info/vb/showthread.php?t=195150

contradictory stance for someone who was once schooled in global jihad and continues to uphold its cause.[170] It is possible that AQIM's statement was also meant, in part, to correct Abu 'Iyad's understanding of the situation in Mali, or perhaps even to rebuke him. Following AQIM's statement, Ansar al-Shari'a was compelled to respond. One of its spokespersons, Muhammad Anis al-Shayib, responded as if he welcomed AQIM's statement, but his response was either wittingly or unwittingly crafted to project rhetorical solidarity and agreement with AQIM without extending a helping hand. He chose to comply not with the call requesting the assistance of "the sons of Tunisia … to repel the onslaught of France," but with the importance of Tunisia's youth not to abandon their country. In his words: "it is incumbent upon Muslim youth of Tunisia and elsewhere not to abandon the scene to the secularists and others who are Westernized so that they may cause havoc and corruption in the land; rather, those who are capable of remaining at home should do so and should struggle against their enemies using proof and the Qur'an."[171]

The level of support in Tunisia for Ansar al-Shari'a is disputed,[172] and while their da'wa activities may continue to yield them popularity if they continue to provide welfare services to the needy,[173] perhaps with the help of donations from abroad,[174] their jihadi identity is ambiguous at best. Can Ansar al-Shari'a continue its strong yet ambiguous jihadi rhetoric without any supporting action? What will it take for them to engage in jihad against the authorities? One would have thought that when the government banned the group from holding its annual meeting in May 2013 in Kairouan,[175] the group would have had reason to

---

[170] Abu 'Iyad al-Tunisi, interview on 30 January 2013.

[171] Cited in *al-Shaab News*, 18 March 2013, http://alshaabnews.net/news/world-news/8483-2013-03-18-15-47-29.html (last accessed 14 May 2013).

[172] See Aaron Zelin, "Meeting Tunisia's Ansar al-Shari'a," *Foreign Policy*, 8 March 2013, http://mideast.foreignpolicy.com/posts/2013/03/08/meeting_tunisias_ansar_al_sharia (last accessed 14 May 2013). Members of Ansar al-Shari'a told Zelin that their movement consists of about 90,000 to 100,000, but, as he himself remarks, that is likely to be an exaggerated figure.

[173] On their website, see "al-Qafila al-Khayriyya al-Thalitha li-Ansar al-Shari'a bi-Hammam al-Aghzaz," *Ansar al-Shari'a bi-Tunis*, 28 April 2013, http://ansar-ashariaa.com/index.php/2013-02-16-22-13-49/2013-02-16-22-21-18/343-2013-05-09-15-03-20 (last accessed 15 May 2013); See also Zelin, "Meeting Tunisia's Ansar al-Shari'a."

[174] Some have alleged external funding from Saudi Arabia, see Muhammad Najib Wahibi, "Ansar al-Shari'a bi-Tunis Dawala Dakhil Dawla?," *al-Hiwar al-Mutamaddin*, 20 February 2013, http://www.ahewar.org/debat/show.art.asp?aid=346499 (last accessed 15 May 2013).

[175] "Tunisia Bars Ansar al-Sharia Salafist meeting in Kairouan," *BBC*, 17 May 2013, http://www.bbc.co.uk/news/world-africa-22578535 (last accessed 4 July 2013).

rally its supporters and engage in violence. Yet Abu 'Iyad settled for the use of sarcastic abuse of the authorities, thanking them for "having committed stupidities" that assisted "in spreading our da'wa."[176]

The group met with further justification to resort to violence when the Tunisian government declared it to be a terrorist group following the assassination of Mohamed Brahmi – leader of the opposition party Movement of the People – in July 2013.[177] However, Abu 'Iyad rushed to deny allegations that his group was responsible for this attack, rebuking the regime for implying that this was the case.[178] The group later released an official statement accusing the government of concocting charges against the group to hide its failures; reiterated its loyalty to Qa'idat al-Jihad while at the same time stressing that it has no ties with it or any foreign group; and made it clear that it would not resort to responses that would cause its members to be dragged into prisons, as befell al-Nahda in the 1990s.[179]

It is clear that the group is willing to undergo considerable cost to avoid giving the government an excuse to imprison its members en masse. If this is the objective of the group, it is going about it the wrong way. The militant worldview Ansar al-Shari'a projects and its support of global jihad is sufficient to allow the government to blame it for terrorist operations regardless of whether it committed them. In colloquial parlance, it is as if Ansar al-Shari'a is asking for it. But is the group intent on developing a clandestine militant program in the long term? If it is, it risks being perceived as a group pursuing a jihadi without jihad formula and might disappoint some of its followers.

---

[176] Abu 'Iyad, speech on the occasion of the third annual meeting of Ansar al-Shari'a, *Ansar al-Shari'a bi-Tunis*, 19 May 2013, http://ansar-ashariaa.com/index.php/2013-02-16-21-33-03/2013-02-16-21-36-58/379-2013-05-20-15-02-05 (last accessed 4 July 2013).
[177] "Tunis Tusannif Ansar al-Shari'a ka-Jama'a 'Irhabiyya'," *BBC*, 27 August 2013, http://www.bbc.co.uk/arabic/middleeast/2013/08/130827_tunisia_ansar.shtml (last accessed 7 October 2013).
[178] Abu 'Iyad, *Ansar al-Shari'a bi-Tunis*, July 2013, http://www.ansar-alsharee3a.com/showthread.php?t=3650 (last accessed 5 August 2013); the group also released an official statement denying the allegations: http://www.ansar-ashariaa.com/index.php/2013-02-16-22-16-41/539-2013-07-27-10-40-14 (last accessed 5 August 2013).
[179] "Bayan min Ansar al-Shari'a bi-Tunis bi-Khusus Idraj al-Tanzim 'ala La'ihat al-Irhab," *Shabakat Shumukh al-Islam*, 3 September 2013, https://shamikh1.info/vb/showthread.php?t=210826 (last accessed 4 September 2013).

EGYPT

If Ansar al-Shari'ia in Tunisia suffers from an inconsistent jihadi ideology that does not support jihad at home and is yet to determine how it could support jihad abroad, the jihadi landscape in Egypt is becoming crowded with new jihadi groups and also suffers from a set of glaring inconsistencies. In Egypt, where virtually uninterrupted peaceful protests beginning on 25 January 2011 led to the fall of Husni Mubarak three weeks later, several jihadi groups have since emerged. As it is the birthplace of Ayman al-Zawahiri, who has been declared by jihadi websites to be Usama Bin Ladin's successor, it was expected that jihadism would have a wider appeal there, posing a serious disruption to the political transition. Further, the ongoing unrests in Egypt, particularly following the military's ousting of the elected President Muhammad Mursi and the appointment of an interim government, could be seen to provide additional opportunities for jihadi groups to engage in violence.

Yet violence in Egypt cannot be attributed solely to the Arab Spring. On the one hand, the bulk of the violence from which Egypt is suffering is emanating from clashes between the security forces and protesters as a result Mursi's downfall.[180] Such action cannot be regarded as jihadi violence as many of the new groups that have emerged since the Arab Spring have refrained from translating their jihadi worldview into action. However, there have been a number of violent attacks in the Sinai Peninsula and, following the ousting of Mursi, these have spread to other parts of Egypt. As will be discussed below, Gaza-based groups have claimed responsibility for carrying out these attacks. That is why assessing jihadi militancy in Egypt since the start of the Arab Spring needs to be analyzed through two different angles: the first is in regard to the Sinai Peninsula, which borders both Israel and the Gaza Strip. Militancy in this area is largely conditioned by Gaza-based militants taking advantage of security holes presented by the fall of Husni Mubarak's regime rather than by Egypt-based groups seeking to implement a jihadi project.

---

[180] See the introduction for discussion about expected violence occurring in countries that undergo regime change, particularly those transitioning from an autocratic regime and seeking to forge a democratic path.

It is to be remembered that by closing its Rafah border crossing with Gaza, Mubarak's regime had been, to use Issandr Al Amrani's words, Israel's "silent partner" in its blockade on Gaza since 2007, an unpopular policy both within and outside Egypt.[181] Following Mubarak's fall, when the transitional military government of Egypt initially reopened the Rafah crossing to Palestinians,[182] Gaza-based militants were quick to make use of the crossing to mount attacks against Israel from the Sinai Peninsula, where a light security presence had been mandated by the Camp David Accords that served as the framework of the peace treaty between Egypt and Israel. The Accords stipulated that only a light Egyptian military presence is to be deployed in the Peninsula, backed by Multinational Forces and Observers (MFO) and civilian police to maintain security.[183] That militancy in the Sinai is not exclusively a local affair is evidenced by the cooperation between Egyptian forces and local tribal leaders who are keen to help establish security between the Peninsula and the Gaza Strip.[184] Local tribal leaders were also reported to have helped to secure the release of seven Egyptian soldiers who were taken hostage in May 2013, even though no specific group responsible for the hostage-taking was identified.[185] It should be added that militants in Sinai have also threatened Hamas' security apparatus in Gaza, and consider Hamas to be as much of an enemy as the "Jewish enemy."[186] Nevertheless, since several groups emerged following the Arab Spring, this section deals with their operational credentials.

---

[181] Issandr El Amrani, "Egypt Confronts its Role in the Gaza Blockade," *Foreign Policy*, 4 June 2010, http://mideast.foreignpolicy.com/posts/2010/06/04/egypt_confronts_its_role_in_the_gaza_blockade (last accessed 14 May 2013). See also David Poort, "History of Israeli Blockade on Gaza," *al-Jazeera*, 2 November 2011, http://www.aljazeera.com/indepth/features/2011/10/20111030172356990380.html (last accessed 15 May 2013).

[182] "Gaza: Egypt 'to open Rafah crossing to Palestinians'", 25 May 2011, *BBC*, http://www.bbc.co.uk/news/world-middle-east-13552685 (last accessed 14 May 2013).

[183] "Camp David Accords," 17 September 1978, see the text of the document on *Israel Ministry of Foreign Affairs*, http://www.mfa.gov.il/mfa/foreignpolicy/peace/guide/pages/camp%20david%20accords.aspx (last accessed 14 May 2013). See also the MFO website http://mfo.org/ for details as to how the MFO came to exist instead of the UN forces as the Accords had initially stipulated. The mandate of MFO, it should be stressed, is an observer force.

[184] "Egypt tribes back offensive against militants in Sinai," *BBC*, 10 August 2012, http://www.bbc.co.uk/news/world-middle-east-19205577 (last accessed 14 May 2013).

[185] "Mursi Yu'akkid lada Istiqbalihi al-Junud al-Mufraj 'anhum anna al-Ifraj Tamma bi-Juhud jami' al-Jihat," *BBC*, 22 May 2013, http://www.bbc.co.uk/arabic/middleeast/2013/05/130522_morsi_receive_released_soldiers.shtml (link accessed on the same day). It should be noted that al-Salafiyy al-Jihadiyya fi Sina' released a statement denying responsibility for the hostages, *Shabakat Ansar al-Mujahidin*, 21 May 2013, http://as-ansar.com/vb/showthread.php?t=89835 (last accessed 22 May 2013).

[186] Isabel Kershner, "Militants in Egyptian Sinai Fire Rockets Into Israel but Do No Damage," *The New York Times*, 17 April 2013, http://www.nytimes.com/2013/04/18/world/middleeast/rockets-fired-from-egyptian-sinai-land-in-israel.html?_r=0 (last accessed 14 May 2013).

The second angle to be analyzed is through Egypt-based new jihadi groups that owe their existence to the Arab Spring. These groups operate in the open and enjoy a wider representation, not least since many of their leaders are not merely vocal through the groups' respective media arms and on jihadi forums, but because they also enjoy the attention of mainstream media, such as al-Jazeera, al-'Arabiyya, and al-Sharq al-Awsat. While their open activities and the media attention they receive provide them with extensive exposure to mainstream Egyptian society, it is also the case that this exposure makes their ideological inconsistencies glaring and subject to greater scrutiny. In what follows, both the Sinai Peninsula and the Egypt-based groups are considered separately.

Sinai Peninsula–Gaza Militants

Following the Arab Spring, several groups emerged that operated largely in the Sinai Peninsula. The jihad of some of these groups does not extend beyond bluster, while others have been operational. Two general remarks are worth highlighting: the first has to do with the fact that active groups did not carry out operations outside Sinai until the ousting of Muhammad Mursi. It is not out of sympathy or loyalty to the Muslim Brotherhood (MB) that they expanded their operations; indeed, they do not consider the MB to be lawful and continue to accuse it of having violated God's Law. Instead, as the Ibn Taymiyya Center for the Media explained in a statement released after Mursi's ousting,[187] jihadis needed to capitalize on this event as an "historical opportunity" to reawaken the *umma*. The statement went on to rally Muslims to fight against the regimes.[188]

Second, it cannot be stated with certainty whether these groups are collaborating with each other. On the one hand, some of the statements published on jihadi websites under the umbrella of a certain *al-Salafiyya al-Jihadiyya fi Sinai* (Salafi-Jihadism in Sinai) are perhaps designed to suggest that the groups in Sinai operate under a unified command. It is not clear whether this is a generic designation for all the groups operating in Sinai or whether it is a separate group. On

---

[187] Markaz Ibn Taymiyya was founded after the "Arab Spring" and it is devoted to publishing materials by jihadi groups in Gaza and Egypt.

[188] Markaz Ibn Taymiyya, "Istinhad al-Umma li-Muwajahat al-Jaysh al-Misri al-'Amil," 23 September 2013, https://shamikh1.info/vb/showthread.php?t=211943 (accessed on the same day).

the other hand, since specific groups are publishing their own founding statements and claiming responsibilities for specific operations, it is doubtful that these groups are acting in concert.

While in its early releases al-Salafiyya al-Jihadiyya in Sinai repeatedly enumerated what it believes to be the Egyptian military's indiscriminate arrests and attacks against the people of Sinai, it did not call on targeting the military and took no responsibility for any of the attacks against it. Indeed, in a September 2012 statement the group asserted that "the Egyptian Army and police are not our military target, our weapons are now directed against the Zionist enemy only."[189] However, the tone of its statements following Mursi's ousting changed. The group highlighted that al-Salafiyya al-Jihadiyya does not stand by Mursi; that his government did not govern according to God's Law; and that it did not claim responsibility for any of the attacks against the military in Sinai or elsewhere. Nonetheless, the group began to exhort Muslims to take up arms against the military. It asserted that Mursi's removal is clear proof that democracy is not the solution and warned that "we shall not stand by with tied hands."[190] Its call for armed struggle was more explicit in a later statement when it claimed that the military's crackdown on the protesters clearly demonstrated "the corruption of the program of those who espouse democracy" and the futility of "the peaceful path" and called on the Muslims of Egypt to fight the regime.[191]

One of the early groups to emerge in the Sinai Peninsula calls itself **Ansar al-Jihad fi Jazirat Sina'**; it released its founding statement on 20 December 2011.[192] The group's statement indicates that it was founded in response to the Egyptian security forces' crackdown on a jihadi cell in Sinai. It is likely that the cell in question is based in Gaza, since several of its members

---

[189] Bayan Al-Salafiyya al-Jihadiyya fi Sina', *Shabakat al-Fida' al-Islamiyya*, 17 September 2012, http://alfidaa.org/vb/showthread.php?t=46583 (last accessed 5 August 2013).
[190] Bayan Al-Salafiyya al-Jihadiyya fi Sina', *Shabakat al-Fida' al-Islamiyya*, 6 July 2013, http://alfidaa.org/vb/showthread.php?t=68525 (last accessed 5 August 2013); Bayan Al-Salafiyya al-Jihadiyya fi Sina', *Shabakat al-Fida' al-Islamiyya*, 3 August 2013, http://alfidaa.org/vb/showthread.php?t=71723&highlight=%D3%ED%E4%C7%C1 (last accessed 5 August 2013).
[191] "Bayanu al-Salafiyya al-Jihadiyya fi Sina': wa-Qatiluhum hatta la Takuna Fitna," 22 August 2013, *Shabakat Shumukh al-Islam*, https://shamikh1.info/vb/showthread.php?t=210103 (accessed on the same day).
[192] *Shabakat Sinam al-Islam*, "al-Bayan al-Ta'sisi," 20 December 2011, http://snam-s.net/vb/showthread.php?t=10607

who were arrested admitted that they belong to Harakat al-Jihad al-Islami in Gaza;[193] but since the leadership of Harakat al-Jihad later denied any involvement in the militant activities in Sinai, it is possible that the militants were acting on their own initiative.[194] They appear to have joined forces with Egyptian militants when they attacked a police station in the city of al-'Arish in the Sinai Peninsula in July 2011;[195] the attack led to the arrest of several members of the cell and the killing of jihadi militant Salim Muhammad Jum'a. The cell does not seem to have been involved in the series of attacks on gas pipelines in Sinai that supply gas to Israel.[196] Salim is hailed not as a member but as a "martyr" in the founding statement of Ansar al-Jihad, and if the statement is correct, the same Salim had participated in an operation in August 2011 near Eilat, an Israeli town bordering Egypt.[197] This indicates that Salim's group predates the founding of Ansar al-Jihad.

The founding statement of Ansar al-Jihad suggests that the group is intent on mounting violent operations. It promises to do its utmost to "fight against the corrupt [Egyptian] regime and its backers the Jews, the Americans and those in their orbit;" the group also projects a global jihadi mission, promising to uphold the oath Usama Bin Ladin once made that "America and its people shall not enjoy security unless we ourselves enjoy security in Palestine and until all unbelieving armies withdraw from the land of Muhammad."[198] To formalize its commitment to global jihad, on 23 January 2012 the group pledged allegiance to Ayman al-Zawahiri, who nonetheless has not yet welcomed the group into the fold, and perhaps never will.[199]

---

[193] Ashraf Suwaylim, 16 August 2011, http://www.masrawy.com/news/egypt/politics/2011/august/16/terrorism.aspx (last accessed 2 March 2013).

[194] Iman Mhanna, 28 December 2012, http://www.youm7.com/News.asp?NewsID=890754

[195] Hatim al-Bilk, 29 July 2011, http://www.deltaelyoum.com/news.php?id=8555 (last accessed 2 March 2013).

[196] Based on media reports, these attacks are "probably the work of restive local Bedouins, who have long felt discriminated against by the Egyptian government, or possibly Palestinian saboteurs," see Isabel Kershner and Mona El-Naggar, "Pipeline Blast in Sinai, Said to Be Sabotage, Cuts Gas Supply in Israel and Jordan," 27 April 2011, http://www.nytimes.com/2011/04/28/world/middleeast/28sinai.html (last accessed 3 March 2013). But the group calling itself Jama'at Ansar Bayt al-Maqdis (Supporters of Jerusalem Group) has claimed responsibility for these attacks. See below.

[197] Yaakov Katz, "7 dead in terror attacks; IDF still looking for terrorists," *Jerusalem Post*, 18 August 2011, http://www.jpost.com/Defense/Article.aspx?id=234334 (last accessed 2 March 2013).

[198] "Ikhwanukum Yubayi'un al-Amir Ayman al-Zawahiri," *Shabakat Shumukh al-Islam*, 23 January 2012, http://www.shamikh1.info/vb/showthread.php?t=145330

[199] *Ibid.*

Yet despite the threatening rhetoric, littered with intentions and promises of militancy, the group has not yet engaged in a single militant operation. Not only is the group inactive on the operational front, it has been slow even to develop a media strategy: as yet, the group does not have its own media outlet, relying instead on a reporter (*murasil*) who posts its statements on jihadi forums.

Another jihadi group, which calls itself **Jund al-Shari'a** and is Sinai-focused, released its founding statement on 30 July 2012. Its pedestrian founding statement is indicative of its status as perhaps the most amateurish of all jihadi groups. It threatened the regime with the "sword" unless its demands are met. It insists that the regime must apply God's Law in Egypt; that it should cease pursuing jihadis in Sinai, release all jihadi prisoners, and end "all the operations by the American occupation forces that claim to be peace keeping forces in Egypt." The last demand is likely a reference to the multinational forces stationed in Sinai under the mandate of the UN as part of the Camp David Accords; in jihadi parlance – and undoubtedly to the surprise of most Americans – the UN and the United States are two sides of the same imperialist coin.

In addition to its ominous threats against the regime, Jund al-Shari'a addressed itself to the "American occupying forces," warning that unless they implement its demands within three days, the United States would regret its decision. The group is sure that the Americans would make note of their threats "for we know that their spies are constantly following the jihadi websites."[200] The three days have long passed and, to date, the group has not mounted any operations against the Egyptian regime or against the "American occupation forces," whichever these are.

The jihadi group **Majlis Shura al-Mujahidin fi Aknaf Bayt al-Maqdis** (Advisory Council of the Jihadis in the Environs of Jerusalem) is one of two groups that are of note from an operational perspective. While it made its operational debut in the Sinai Peninsula, it is a Gaza-based group

---

[200] "al-Bayan al-Ta'sisi li-Jund al-Shari'a," *Shabakat Ansar al-Mujahidin*, 30 July 2012, http://www.as-ansar.com/vb/showthread.php?s=e61601e464c2af8493bb...

and some of its strategically oriented literature is largely addressed to Gazans.[201] As such, it does not qualify as part of the new jihadi landscape in Egypt, but it is included in this section because it conducted operations in Sinai. Unlike the previous two groups, which are big on propaganda and short on militant action, Majlis Shura al-Mujahidin appears to have sought to demonstrate its commitment to jihad through deeds. Its founding statement is dated May 2012, but it was not released until June, along with an additional statement announcing its responsibility for an operation in Sinai. The group quickly established a link with Markaz Ibn Taymiyya li-al-I'lam to release its publications, a media arm that was founded in December 2011 following the Arab Spring.[202]

Majlis Shura al-Mujahidin sees itself responding to the events of the Arab Spring, particularly the fall of several dictators "to prepare for the next phase … for there is no place today for patriotism, nationalism, secularism and democracy. Rather this is the Muslims' battle to reclaim God's Law on earth, the glories of the *umma* and its dominion over humanity so that God's Law may reign supreme. "[203] The group's mission statement goes on to add that its "foundation for a jihadi path" is part of a "global project that seeks to re-establish the Caliphate." It is in this global spirit that it released a statement eulogizing Abu Yahya al-Libi – who was killed in June 2012 by a US drone strike – while welcoming the killing of the U.S. Ambassador in Libya Chris Stevens.[204]

But the bulk of Majlis Shura al-Mujahidin's threats is directed against "the Jews, God's enemies," threatening Israelis that "what awaits you is different from the past … for the era of negotiations, truces, and half solutions is gone."[205] True to its promises, the group mounted a

[201] See, for example, Abu Bilal al-Shami, *Tawjihat Manhajiyya li-al-Salafiyya al-Jihadiyya fi Aknaf Bayt al-Maqdis*, posted 10 April 2013 on *al-Fida'*, http://snam-s.net/vb/showthread.php?t=10607 (last accessed 15 May 2013).
[202] "I'lam al-Anam bi-Intilaq Markaz Ibn Taymiyya li-al-I'lam," *Shabakat al-Jihad al-I'lami*, 21 December 2011, http://www.aljahad.com/vb/showthread.php?t=14712
[203] "I'lam al-Muwahhidin bi-Tashkil Majlis Shura al-Mujahidin fi Aknaf Bayt al-Maqdis," *Shabakat Ansar al-Mujahidin*, 19 June 2012, http://as-ansar.com/vb/showthread.php?t=64109 (last accessed 3 March 2013).
[204] Majlis Shura al-Mujahidin, "Ta'ziya," Statement no. 17, 19 September 2012, *Shabakat Ansar al-Mujahidin*, http://as-ansar.com/vb/showthread.php?t=71171 (last accessed 3 March 2013).
[205] "I'lam al-Muwahhidin bi-Tashkil Majlis Shura al-Mujahidin fi Aknaf Bayt al-Maqdis," *Shabakat Ansar al-Mujahidin*, 19 June 2012, http://as-ansar.com/vb/showthread.php?t=64109 (last accessed 3 March 2013).

cross-border attack, claiming that it targeted two Israeli patrol units,[206] and in the video that it released detailing the operation, a member proclaimed that it is a gift to Ayman al-Zawahiri.[207] Two members, a Saudi and an Egyptian, carried out this mission. It should be noted that the media reported that the target was not two Israeli patrol units, but a "convoy of construction workers" building a security fence along Israel's border with Egypt.[208]

It is evident that Majlis Shura al-Mujahidin's operational credentials made an impression on Ayman al-Zawahiri. On 5 August 2012, Markaz Ibn Taymiyya released a statement announcing the release of a certain Hisham al-Sa'aydni, known as Abu al-Walid al-Maqdisi, of Palestinian origin, and who had been imprisoned by Hamas for nearly two years.[209] Soon thereafter, on 16 October, Majlis Shura al-Mujahidin released a statement announcing Abu al-Walid's martyrdom along with that of Abu al-Bara' Ashraf, describing them as "the elites of the group's religious scholars, leaders and mujahidin."[210] The two were killed by an Israeli aerial offensive in Gaza. On 30 November 2012, al-Zawahiri released a statement eulogizing Hisham al-Sa'aydni, indicating a clear display of his approval of the group's activities.[211] Although al-Zawahiri did not mention the full name of the group, he did refer to the latter part of it (aknaf bayt al-Maqdis), a reference that he used in a subsequent statement released in April 2013.[212] Although it would be tempting to speculate as to whether al-Zawahiri's use of the expression *aknaf bayt al-Maqdis* is an explicit endorsement of the group, it is also the case that this is an

[206] David D. Kirpatrick, "Sinai Group Claims Role in Attack on Israel," *The New York Times*, 23 September 2012, http://www.nytimes.com/2012/09/24/world/middleeast/sinai-militants-claim-role-in-israel-border-attack.html (last accessed 3 March 2013).

[207] Majlis Shura al-Mujahidin, "Wa-Irta'adat al-Yahud li-Qurbi al-Wu'ud," YouTube: http://www.youtube.com/watch?v=1IvPaUK2KIk (last accessed 6 March 2013).

[208] See "Deadly Attack on Israel-Egypt Border," *BBC*, 18 June 2012, http://www.bbc.co.uk/news/world-middle-east-18483018 (last accessed 3 March 2013).

[209] Markaz Ibn Taymiyya li-al-I'lam, "Tahni'at ahl al-Tawhid bi-Fakak Asr al-Sheikh Hisham al-S'aydni, *Shabakat Ansar al-Mujahidin*, 5 August 2012, http://as-ansar.com/vb/showthread.php?t=67684

[210] Majlis Shura al-Mujahidin, "Majlis Shura al-Mujahidin Yahtasibu 'Inda Allah Qa'idayn," *Shabakat Ansar al-Mujahidin*, 16 October 2012, http://as-ansar.com/vb/showthread.php?t=72779

[211] Ayman al-Zawahiri, "Ratha' al-Sheikh Abi Muhammad al-Maqdisi," *Shabakat Ansar al-Mujahidin*, 30 November 2012, http://as-ansar.com/vb/showthread.php?t=75824&highlight=%C7%E1%D3%DA%ED%C...

[212] Ayman al-Zawahiri, "Tawhid al-Kalima hawla Kalimat al-Tawhid," *Shabakat al-Fida' al-Islamiyya*, posted 10 April 2013, http://alfidaa.org/vb/showthread.php?t=60873 (last accessed 14 May 2013).

expression used by many to designate historical Palestine, and al-Zawahiri himself had on many occasions used it long before the group emerged on the scene.[213]

It is worth noting that the group's media bureau released a statement denying responsibility for the attack that resulted in the death of Egyptian soldiers in Sinai on 5 August 2012, of which they were accused by some media outlets.[214] Even after the ousting of Mursi, the group resisted attacking the Egyptian military. For example, when an Israeli drone targeted militants in Sinai in August 2013, the group accused the Egyptian military for conspiring with Israeli forces to carry out the attack, but insisted that this attack should serve as a reminder to Egyptians that the "Jews" who "occupy Palestine" are "their prime enemy."[215] Within days, the group claimed responsibility for an attack on Eilat in retaliation.[216]

As observed earlier, the ousting of the Muslim Brotherhood in July 2013 led to an increase in attacks that have not been limited to the Sinai. The most active group mounting operations against the Egyptian military, in revenge for what it considers to be its persecution of Muslims is **Jama'at Ansar Bayt al-Maqdis** (Supporters of Jerusalem Group). Even though the latter part of the name may lead one to confuse it with Majlis Shura al-Mujahidin, it is a different group. Even members on jihadi forums are confused as to the identity of this group and whether it is related to Majlis Shura al-Mujahidin.[217]

Like Majlis Shura al-Mujahidin, the group is also based in Gaza, and it is likely that it is the same group that pre-dates the Arab Spring and once operated under the name "Jama'at Ansar

---

[213] Ayman al-Zawahiri, "Asas al-Islah," 2005, it can be accessed on *Jihad Archive*, https://www.jarchive.net/details.php?item_id=982 (last accessed 15 May 2013).
[214] Majlis Shura al-Mujahidin, "Bayan Nafi Ayy Silat bi-Maqtal al-Junud al-Misriyyin," *Shabakat Ansar al-Mujahidin*, 6 August 2012, http://as-ansar.com/vb/showthread.php?t=67795
[215] Majlis Shura al-Mujahidin, "Bayanun Hawla al-Ghara al-Yahudiyya 'ala Ardi Sina'," *Shabakat al-Fida' al-Islamiyya*, 8 August 2013, http://alfidaa.org/vb/showthread.php?t=72458 (accessed on the same day).
[216] Majlis Shura al-Mujahidin, "Majlis Shura al-Mujahidin Yaqsifu Umm al-Rashshash 'Eilat' bi-Sarukhi Grad," 13 August 2013, *Shabakat al-Fida' al-Islamiyya*, http://alfidaa.org/vb/showthread.php?t=72693 (accessed on the same day).
[217] "Tasa'ul 'an Jama'ati Ansar Bayt al-Maqdis," *Shabakat al-Fida' al-Islamiyya*, 2 October 2013, http://alfidaa.org/vb/showthread.php?t=76811 (accessed on the same day).

al-Sunna – Aknaf Bayt al-Maqdis." The latter had been active as early as January 2010,[218] and in June the same year the group began publishing on two jihadi forums and released a statement introducing the group.[219] The last statement released by the group under this name was in August 2011; soon thereafter, in September, the same forum member who had been publishing its statements began to publish statements under the new name Jama'at Aknaf Bayt al-Maqdis.

From an operational perspective, the group has distinguished itself from Majlis Shura al-Mujahidin by claiming responsibility for attacks not just against Israel, but also against the Egyptian military. It has claimed responsibility for launching numerous rocket attacks against Israel,[220] and since the ousting of Mursi it has been claiming responsibility for attacks inside Egypt. The group has documented what it considers to be indiscriminate attacks by the Egyptian military against several villages in Sinai,[221] and claims to have mounted several operations against the Egyptian military in response.[222] Among others, in September 2013 the group claimed responsibility for the attack against the Egyptian Interior Minister, and apologized to the public for not having killed him. The group did not consider its attack to be in support of the Muslim Brotherhood, although some on jihadi forums wondered whether the group was connected, considering its intensified attacks, particularly following the ousting of Mursi. Instead, the group declared that its operations are in solidarity with Muslims who were attacked in mosques and were arrested or killed because of their loyalty to Islam.[223]

---

[218] One of its early (possibly earliest) statements was posted on 10 January 2010 and may be accessed on Shabakat al-Shumukh al-Islamiyya, https://shamikh1.info/vb/showthread.php?t=56512&highlight=%C3%DF%E4%C7%DD (last accessed 8 October 2013).

[219]*Shabakat Shumukh al-Islam*, posted 15 June 2013, https://shamikh1.info/vb/showthread.php?t=64512 (last accessed 8 October 2013).

[220] Among others, see Majlis Shura al-Mujahidin, "al-Hamla al-Sarukhiyya," *Shabakat Ansar al-Mujahidin*, Bayan no. 30, 21 November2012, http://as-ansar.com/vb/showthread.php?t=75264; "Qasf Madinat Umm al-Rashrash al-Muhtalla 'Eilat' bi-Sarukhayn Grad," *al-Shumukh*, 17 April 2013, https://shamikh1.info/vb/showthread.php?t=198404 (last accessed 15 May 2013).

[221] Ansar Bayt al-Maqdis, "al-Jaysh al-Misri 'Amala wa-Ijram," 11 September 2013, *Shabakat Shumukh al-Islam*, https://shamikh1.info/vb/showthread.php?t=211225 (accessed on the same day); "al-Bayanu al-Thani bi-Khususi al-Hamlat al-'Askariyya al-Muwassa'a 'ala Ahali Sina': Wa-Yastamirru al-Ijram," 15 September 2013, *Shabakat Shumukh al-Islam*, https://shamikh1.info/vb/showthread.php?t=211444 (accessed on the same day).

[222] See for example its claim of responsibility for the Egyptian security base in southern Sinai, Ansar Bayt al-Maqdis, "I'lanu Mas'uliyyatuna 'an Istihdafi Mudiriyyati Amn Janubi Sina'", 9 October 2013, *Shabakat al-Fida' al-Islamiyya*, http://alfidaa.org/vb/showthread.php?t=77522 (accessed on the same day).

[223] Ansar Bayt al-Maqdis, "Ghazwatu al-Tha'ri li-Muslimi Misr," *Shabakat Shumukh al-Islam*, 8 September 2013, https://shamikh1.info/vb/showthread.php?t=211080 (accessed on the same day). Among other noteworthy attacks,

Egypt-Based Groups

Other groups that owe their existence to the Arab Spring have emerged elsewhere in Egypt. Like Ansar al-Shari'a in Tunisia, new jihadi groups in Egypt seek to project a jihadi worldview. But whereas in Tunisia Ansar al-Shari'a can lay claim to the "Salafi movement" (*al-tayyar al-salafi*) to justify its religious credentials as incorruptible in the face of positive law, the "Salafi" terrain in Egypt is occupied by a variety of groups including those that formed political parties, contested elections and claimed almost 25 per cent of the seats in Parliament.[224] Thus, it is all the more important that the new groups should distinguish themselves by their jihadi, not just their Salafi credentials.

Indeed, the expression *"al-tayyar al-jihadi"* (the jihadi movement) is used liberally in Egypt to designate the new jihadi groups. Their various leaders all agree that the post-revolution regime compromises God's Law. In the words of Muhammad al-Zawahiri – Ayman's brother and one of the most vocal spokespeople who owes his current public role to the prisoners' release following the Arab Spring – "the political situation in Egypt, in our view, transgresses God's Law; that is why we call on utilizing the correct lawful means to exercise politics guided by [Islamic] Law."[225] He is also on record stating that the movement's mission is "not just jihad, but also to deliver people from the darkness [of injustice] to the light [of divine justice]" and those who come in the way of implementing this mission "ought to be removed by force."[226] In other words, if one were to understand Muhammad al-Zawahiri's stance by the standards of

---

the group claimed responsibility for the assassination of Muhammad Mabrouk, an Egyptian lieutenant colonel tasked with combating the activities of religious extremist groups, "I'lanu Mas'uliyyatina 'an Ightiyali al-Mujrimi Muhammad Mabrouk," *Shabakat al-Fida' al-Islamiyya*, 19 November 2013, http://alfidaa.org/vb/showthread.php?t=82470 (accessed on the same day). It also claimed responsibility for targeting the Egyptian airforce intelligence base in Isma'iliyya and called on "our people in Egypt to stay away from all military and police bases for they are lawful targets of the mujahidin," "I'lanu Mas'uliyyatina 'an Istihdafi al-Mukhabarati al-Harbiyyat bi-al-Isma'iliyya," *Shabakat al-Fida' al-Islamiyya*, 21 October 2013, http://alfidaa.org/vb/showthread.php?t=78975 (accessed on the same day).

[224] Stephane Lacroix, 'Sheikhs and Politicians: Inside the New Egyptian Salafism,' *Foreign Policy at Brookings*, June 2012.

[225] Interview with Muhammad al-Zawahiri by Walid 'Abd al-Rahman, "Shaqiq Za'im Tanzim al-Qa'ida: al-Wad' al-Siyasi fi Misr 'Mukhali li-Shar' Alla'," *al-Sharq al-Awsat*, 28 February 2013, Issue 12480.

[226] See interview with Muhammad al-Zawahiri with the television show "al-Irhabi," link available on *al-Yawm al-Sabi'*, 25 April 2013, http://www.youm7.com/News.asp?NewsID=1035943 (last accessed 16 May 2013).

traditional jihadi discourse, one would have to surmise that jihad is a lawful means by which to pursue the implementation of God's Law.

Muhammad al-Zawahiri is one of many who are considered to be representatives of this post-Arab Spring jihadi movement in Egypt. While he was once involved with founding a group by the name *al-Ta'ifa al-Mansura* (the saved sect [destined for paradise]),[227] in later public statements he seems to have distanced himself from its formation, asserting that he does not consider himself to be part of a specific group, and that the movement of which he is a part is "integral to the fabric of this *umma*." He has participated in many conferences organized by several recently formed groups.

Like their Tunisian counterparts, new Egyptian groups are unremitting when it comes to proclaiming their commitment to a jihadi worldview. While they deny any organizational links with al-Qa'ida, they support the causes it champions, and some of their members are said to be fighting in Syria.[228] Also like their Tunisian counterparts, they do not actively practice jihad, even when they cite persecution by the regime's security agencies;[229] further, this inconsistency is even more glaring when their leaders laud the obligation of jihad to implement God's Law – on the one hand – and in the same sentence decry as slander rumors that accuse them of making force against the regime part of their agenda.

The groups Jam'iyyat Ansar al-Shari'a and al-Tali'a al-Salafiyya al-Mujahida – Ansar al-Shari'a seem to enjoy more attention than others, at least in the mainstream media.[230] It should be noted that the agenda of the different groups in Egypt are not always distinct, for while different groups with their own media outlets have been formed, it is not unusual for leaders of different

---

[227] See interview with Muhammad al-Zawahiri on *Shabakat al-Yaqin*, available on YouTube: http://www.youtube.com/watch?v=B9Y6IckO9Oc (last accessed 17 May 2013).
[228] One of the participants of *Shabakat Ansar al-Mujahidin* reports that a certain "hero" by the name Mu 'adh al-Albani, "a student of knowledge in Ansar al-Shari'a in Egypt was martyred in Syria," posted on 28 February 2013, http://www.as-ansar.com/vb/showthread.php?t=82720 (last accessed 17 May 2013).
[229] See interview with Abu Khadra about a siege by security forces on a mosque in December 2012, https://www.youtube.com/watch_popup?v=O3z1E8SSD3E (last accessed 17 May 2013).
[230] Other less known groups have also emerged: al-Haraka al-Islamiyya li-Tatbiq al-Shari'a (Ansar al-Haqq), with a website http://www.sharyaa.com/index.php and a Facebook page https://www.facebook.com/shary3aa (last accessed 17 May 2013). Its first statement on the occasion of France's intervention in Mali suggests that the group may be a coalition of various jihadi groups in Egypt.

groups to release joint statements. It is not yet clear whether the multiplicity of groups is due to routine and expected decentralization that accompanies the building of a social movement, or whether it is due to competition for leadership among those who proclaim the same cause.

Jam'iyyat Ansar al-Shari'a is led by a certain Sayyid Abu Khadra, and given that Muhammad al-Zawahiri has featured in many of the group's organized conferences and lectures – many of them are posted on YouTube – it obviously enjoys his endorsement. The group was formed at the latest by April 2012;[231] it has a website,[232] a Facebook page for its leader,[233] and a media arm.[234] Its main public statements and the articulation of its views are for the most part communicated through lectures posted on the group's own YouTube page and on Abu Khadra's Facebook page. The earliest video posted by the group dates back to September 2012, condemning the film *The Innocence of Muslims*, which caused outrage in the Muslim world and beyond.[235]

The group's jihadi worldview is explicit and is integral to its *da'wa* mission. In an interview with al-Jazeera, the group's leader Abu Khadra explains that as far as the jihadi movement is concerned "jihad is not just an idea, but it is a definite [Islamic] legal obligation."[236] Given that his group disapproves of the current Egyptian regime, one would expect that this "legal obligation" should be put to use to change the situation. Yet in the same interview, when asked what his movement would do if its demands continue to be ignored by the political establishment, Abu Khadra wholly reversed his position, distancing his group entirely from any intention of conducting militant jihadi actions: "we shall use all means [to pursue our mission], that is, without resorting to raising arms." When pushed further by the interviewer as to whether "it is possible that the group would resort to violence against government security

[231] The Facebook page for the group's media arm Mu'assasat al-Nusra al-I'lamiyya dates 12 April 2012.

[232] Jam'iyyat Ansar al-Shari'a, http://www.ansar-alshari3a.com/index.php (last accessed 16 May 2013). While the website is functioning, at the time of writing this report, it did not have any articles or literature posted.

[233] Sayyid Abu Khadra, *Facebook*, https://www.facebook.com/sayed1abo1akhadra

[234] *Mu'assasat al-Nusra al-I'lamiyya*, http://alnusramedia.blogspot.com/2013/03/blog-post_8225.html

[235] Ansar al-Shari'a, http://www.youtube.com/user/alnusramadia?feature=watch

[236] Abu Khadra, *al-Jazeera*, 29 September 2013, http://www.youtube.com/watch?feature=player_embedded&v=o_h9RSGopVA (last accessed 16 May 2013).

agencies if your demands are not seriously addressed?" Abu Khadra was categorical: "of course not; this matter is not currently on our agenda."[237]

Another familiar group in Egypt, **al-Tali 'a al-Salafiyya al-Mujahida – Ansar al-Shari'a**, released its founding statement in November 2012. The group largely consists of former members of al-Jama'a al-Islamiyya,[238] many of whom had been serving prison sentences and were released following the Arab Spring. It is led by Ahmad 'Ashoush, who was himself in prison prior to the Arab Spring. The group is vocal largely due to its media outreach: it retains its own media arm, Mu'assassat al-Bayan al-I'lamiyya, and it also releases public statements through Mu'assassat al-Faruq li-al-Intaj al-I'lami, which was founded following the Arab Spring and is devoted to the news of Egypt.[239] It also maintains a Facebook page and a twitter account.[240] Beyond its media arms on jihadi forums, members of the group are also vocal in the mainstream media and engage in televised debates with political opponents. They clearly feel at ease being part of the political landscape of Egyptian society: they deliver speeches in Tahrir Square, and Ahmad 'Ashoush gives sermons in mosques. In one of his public statements, Ayman al-Zawahiri used footage from a video in which four members of the group appear in Tahrir Square and he mentions 'Ashoush by name, citing his writings.[241]

Like Ansar al-Shari'a, al-Tali'a al-Salafiyya al-Mujahida calls for the establishment of an Islamic state to implement God's Law. The group is not content with merely providing Islamic legal proofs to justify the necessity of applying the Law: it is also keen to display a level of erudition in Western political philosophy in order to reveal the ingrained atheism in constitutions and

---

[237] Abu Khadra, *al-Jazeera*, 29 September 2013.

[238] For an insider's look on the groups, see Muntasir al-Zayyat, *al-Jama'a al-Islamiyya: Ru'ya min al-Dakhil*, Cairo: Dar Misr al-Mahrusa, 2nd edition, 2005.

[239] "al-Bayan al-Ta'sisi li-Mu'assasat al-Faruq," *Shabakat al-Jihad al-'Alami*, http://www.aljahad.com/vb/showthread.php?t=15051

[240] https://twitter.com/Ansarshare3a (last accessed 17 May 2013).

[241] Ayman al-Zawahiri, Risalat al-Amal wa-al-Bishr, (11), http://as-ansar.com/vb/showthread.php?t=73633&highlight=%DA%D4%E6%D4

laws legislated by humans. 'Ashoush published a series of essays that deal with Western social contract theorists, devoting discussions to the writings of Hobbes, Locke and Rousseau.[242]

Beyond its anti-democratic and anti-secular rhetoric, the group seeks to project a staunchly and unapologetically jihadi worldview. For example, when 'Ashoush was asked if Egyptian Salafi-Jihadism is an extension of al-Qa'ida, he passionately responded:

> First, I would like to correct the [common] perception of the organization al-Qa'ida, I would like to give it a more expressive title. I shall therefore call it "the house of honor" (*bayt al-sharaf*), "the title of glory" (*'unwan al-majd*), "home to the dignity of the umma" (*mawtin 'izzat al-umma*). It is a trustworthy entity [that took it upon itself to safeguard] the capabilities of Muslims when it comes to challenging rulers who are [in the business] of selling their people for the cheapest of prices.[243] We must salute Bin Ladin in his lifetime and in his death. If the Arab Spring revolutions were fair, they would have taken Bin Ladin as a symbol of heroism, devotion and sacrifice … we would be honored to be an extension of the organization al-Qa'ida in its *creed, principles and ideas* [emphasis added]. [After all] the organization al-Qa'ida is but an extension of Egyptian jihad, for it was the latter's leaders who founded the organization, among them Sheikh 'Ali al-Rashidi known as Abu 'Ubayda al-Banshiri, and Sheikh Subhi Abu Sitta known as Abu Hifs al-Misri.[244]

Despite the apparent bravado by 'Ashoush, the reader should pay attention not just to what he is saying but also to what he is not saying. 'Ashoush, for example, states: "we would be honored to be an extension of the organization al-Qa'ida," suggesting that it is an aspirational title and speaks of "*imtidad*" (extension), but not of "'*alaqa tanzimiyya*" (an organizational relationship): the former should be understood as figurative, whereas the latter would tie him to

---

[242] Links to these essays can be found on *Shabakat al-Ansar al-Mujahidin*, http://as-ansar.com/vb/search.php?searchid=129780 (last accessed 17 May 2013).

[243] The original Arabic is awkward/weak, hence the awkward expression in the English translation.

[244] Ahmed 'Ashoush, see the full interview on Shabakat Ansar al- Mujahidin, http://www.as-ansar.com/vb/showthread.php?t=73668 (last accessed 17 May 2013). In relation to the founders of AQ, see Nelly Lahoud, *Beware of Imitators*, 4 June 2012, CTC Report, p. 66.

the organization – if al-Qa'ida were to mount and claim responsibility for an attack in Egypt, 'Ashoush would be implicated in it. More importantly, he claims that it is al-Qa'ida's "creed, principles and ideas," but not its "'amaliyyat" (militant operations) or "a'mal (activities) that the Egyptian Salafi-Jihadi movement is honored to be an extension of.

The jihadi worldview of al-Tali'a is ambiguous in other respects. The group's published literature is keen to stress that its objectives in Egypt are to be pursued through preaching and public outreach. For instance, it presents itself as a "missionary movement" and its struggle is pursued "through words and spears"; but whereas in jihadi parlance one expects to read the expression "jihad al-anzima" (Fighting against the regimes), the group is careful to use the expression "muqawamat al-anzima" (resisting the regimes). In spite of its aura of militancy, the group lacks an operational arm. Members of the group called for bombing the pyramids and the sphinx of Giza (abu al-hawl),[245] but none of them has volunteered to carry out this task. Even though the group declared Egypt's first democratically elected President Muhammad Mursi to be "an unlawful ruler" (*hakim ghayr shar'i*), it opted to focus its jihadi priority against the "far enemy," namely Syria. Indeed, one of its leaders, Jalal al-Din Abu al-Futuh, calls on Muslims in general and the youth in particular to join the fight in Syria, proclaiming that "[jihad in] Syria is a path to paradise."[246]

By the time Egypt underwent its second "revolution" in July 2013, the new jihadis in Egypt did not appear to be interested in joining the conflict. When it was announced that a march was set for 30 June, Muhammad al-Zawahiri declared that his movement would not be partisan; he called on both sides to restrain themselves but warned that whoever shed the blood of Muslims would be punished according to the dictates of the Shari'a.[247] The blood of Muslims was shed, and yet Muhammad did not call for jihad. Instead, on 11 July 2013, a week following Mursi's removal, he circulated a proposal "to resolve the crisis." He called on everyone, in particular the

---

[245] http://www.youtube.com/watch?v=oH9Kf2BErZU
[246] Jalal Abu al-Futuh, "Suriya Tariq ila al-Janna," *Shabakat Al-Jihad al-'Alami*, posted on 3 March 2012, http://www.aljahad.info/vb/showthread.php?t=16961 (last accessed 17 May 2013).
[247] Interview with Muhammad al-Zawahiri, 14 June 2013, http://www.youtube.com/watch?v=J7f2txfixXQ (last accessed 4 July 2013).

MB, to accept the ousting of Mursi in return for the complete application of God's Law.[248] His *peaceful* jihadi stance did not stop Egyptian authorities from arresting him as part of the intense crackdown on the Muslim Brotherhood.[249] It was reported that he had been collaborating with the Muslim Brotherhood and even receiving money from the group, accusations that he vehemently denied.[250]

In view of increased attacks in Egypt since the unrest that led to the ousting of Muhammad Mursi jihadism in Egypt associated with Gaza-based groups cannot be dismissed or considered to follow a *jihadis without jihad* formula. Nevertheless, in considering whether there is a causal link between the Arab Spring and jihadism, one cannot ignore that the intensity of the attacks by jihadi groups is less a result of the Arab Spring and more a consequence of a pause in its momentum.

LIBYA

Unlike Tunisia and Egypt, where strictly peaceful protests brought down Zayn al-Din b. 'Ali and Husni Mubarak (then Muhammad Mursi), Libya's revolution was marked by violence that led to an external military intervention before Mu'ammar Qadhafi was ousted and killed. What began as a peaceful "Day of Rage" in February 2011 across different parts of Libya was soon met with violence – including airstrike reprisals – by the government. In response, militant groups were quickly formed, and some of those who fought are reported to have been former jihadis;[251] when the "no-fly zone" mandated by UN Resolution 1973 did not prove sufficient to protect civilians,[252] the United States and European forces launched a military campaign under the UN mandate against government targets, with NATO assuming command of the operation.

---

[248] Muhammad al-Zawahiri, "al-Azma al-Haliyya wa-Subul al-Khuruj al-Shar'iyya minha," *Shabakat al-Fida' al-Islamiyya*, 11 July 2013, http://alfidaa.org/vb/showthread.php?t=69164&highlight=%C7%E1%C3%D2%E3%C9 (last accessed 5 August 2013).

[249] "Egypt crisis: Cairo mosque 'cleared' after siege," *BBC*, 17 August 2013, http://www.bbc.co.uk/news/world-middle-east-23739535.

[250] Muhammad al-Zawahiri, "Radd Muhammad al-Zawahiri 'ala Ittihamat wa-Iftira' at Wasa'il al-I'lam," *Shabakat Shumukh al-Islam*, https://shamikh1.info/vb/showthread.php?t=210152 (accessed 23 August 2013). The statement by Muhammad al-Zawahiri was released on 7 August, ten days before he was arrested.

[251] Alison Pargeter, "Islamist Militant Groups in Post-Qadhafi Libya," *CTC Sentinel*, 20 February 2013, http://www.ctc.usma.edu/posts/islamist-militant-groups-in-post-qadhafi-libya (last accessed 18 May 2013).

[252] United Nations Security Council Resolution 1973, 'No Fly Zone' over Libya. March 17, 2011, http://www.un.org/News/Press/docs/2011/sc10200.doc.htm#Resolution.

Thus, even though Libya's revolution began as a peaceful endeavor, as Alison Pargeter remarks, "Islamist militant elements in Libya have a legitimacy born out of the position that they played in the struggle."[253]

Not only does Libya's militant path to its Arab Spring make it stand out in relation to Tunisia and Egypt, but the weak security apparatus of its transitional government's central authority has blurred the boundaries of legitimacy between militias and government forces. Indeed, many militias, including Islamist ones, have secured the support of government officials to play a law enforcement role, combating narcotic trafficking and crime.[254] The number of these militias and the ideological differences between the Islamist ones are difficult to determine even for observers of Libya's militant landscape.

It is with the above considerations in mind that the militant context of Libya should be analyzed. While militant groups, including those projecting a jihadi worldview, have proliferated since the Arab Spring, and their violent activities are of serious concern to Libya's weak government and its people, the nature of the violence is not in the traditional jihadi style. For example, the militias that attacked government buildings in April 2013, including the foreign and justice ministries, did not call for the application of God's Law, but for the removal of what they believe to be elements that were once in Qadhafi's circle.[255] Some among them are demanding that they be paid salaries that they believe the government has been withholding in order to weaken the militias.[256] Even the kidnapping of the Libyan Prime Minister 'Ali Zaydan on 10 October 2013 is caught within the context of these dynamics. The group that kidnapped the Prime Minister justified it on the basis that the United States' arrest of Abu Anas al-Libi, a

---

[253] Pargeter, "Islamist Militant Groups in Post-Qadhafi Libya."
[254] See for example Peter Fragiskatos, "Disarming Libya's Militia," *BBC*, 27 September 2012, http://www.bbc.co.uk/news/world-africa-19744593 (last accessed 18 May 2013); Jamie Dettmer, "Libyan Government Turns to Ansar Al-Sharia Militia for Crime-Fighting Help," *BBC*, 26 February 2013, http://www.thedailybeast.com/articles/2013/02/25/libyan-government-turns-to-ansar-al-sharia-militia-for-crime-fighting-help.html (last accessed 18 May 2013).
[255] See "Azmat al-Kharijiyya al-Libiyya," *BBC*, 29 April 2013, http://www.bbc.co.uk/arabic/middleeast/2013/04/130429_libya_latest.shtml (last accessed 18 May 2013).
[256] Rana Jawad, "Hal al-Milishiyat al-Musallah Shawka fi Zahr al-Hukuma al-Libiyya?," *BBC*, 2 May 2013.

former al-Qa'ida member, was conducted with the knowledge of the Libyan government.[257] However, subsequent developments suggest that the kidnapping was a result of political rivalries inside the Libyan government. On 21 October, 'Abd al-Mun'im al-Sayyid, the director of the Combating Crimes Bureau, admitted that he had ordered the kidnapping and accused Zaydan of being involved in corruption and drug-related cases.[258]

In the midst of such weak central authority, militias with Islamist and jihadi leanings are carving out a niche for themselves by fighting crime and providing security services, with the blessing of government officials.[259]

It is through this complex and ambiguous lens that Libya's infamous Ansar al-Shari'a and its jihadi worldview can be understood. Following the fall of Qadhafi, in February 2012 a jihadi forum with the username al-Fata al-Muslim posted a message on the jihadi forum *Shabakat al-Fida' al-Islamiyya* calling for the establishment of a group possessing facilities capable of supporting media, military, intelligence and welfare programs. The same username also suggested that the name of such a group be *Ansar al-Shari'a al-Islamiyya*.[260] Soon thereafter, militant groups protested on the streets displaying firearms, raising the Islamic black flag and delivering speeches calling for the application of Shari'a. On jihadi forums this was considered to be the first gathering of those seeking to support Shari'a (*al-multaqa al-awwal li-nusrat al-shari'a*): in other words, Libya's own Ansar al-Shari'a.

For several months little was known regarding the group's platform: it lacked a founding statement or a media arm representing it in jihadi forums. When the U.S. Ambassador in Libya

[257] The Libyan government denied knowledge of the operation, but Secretary of State John Kerry explained that the Libyan government had been informed.
[258] See "Ra'isu Maktabi Mukafahati al-Jarima al-Libi Y'linu Mas'uliyyatahu 'ani 'al-Qabdi' 'ala Ra'isi al-Wuzara'i 'Ali Zaydan," *BBC*, 21 October 2013, http://www.bbc.co.uk/arabic/middleeast/2013/10/131021_libya_pm_kidnapping_responsibility.shtml (accessed the same day).
[259] Abigail Hauslohner, "Islamist Militia Edging Back to Benghazi," *The Washington Post*, 16 February 2013, http://articles.washingtonpost.com/2013-02-16/world/37133600_1_rafallah-al-sahati-islamist-militia-ansar-al-sharia (last accessed 18 May 2013).
[260] Al-Fata al-Muslim, "Hadha huwa al-Waqt al-Munasib li-Zuhur Rayat Jihadiyya fi Libya, Hayya ya Ansar al-Shari'a," *Shabakat al-Fida' al-Islamiyya*, 11 February 2012, text available in CTC Library.

Chris Stevens was killed, the group was widely accused of being behind it,[261] but a spokesperson for the group appeared on YouTube denying responsibility for the attack. Even though the group never admitted responsibility for the killing, angry Libyans attacked Ansar al-Shari'a's base, and for months the group avoided public exposure. At one point it was reported that the group Al-Tajammu' al-Islami li-Tahkim al-Shari'a, which was founded in October 2012, is none other than Ansar al-Shari'a, which decided to relinquish violence and engage in da'wa activities.[262]

But as of January 2013, Ansar al-Shari'a has returned with a more confident and clearer public presence. It released a founding statement detailing its creed and its program; and it also maintains Facebook pages for the group and for its media arm. In addition to proclaiming basic religious principles, such as "the return to the teachings of the Book," the group's founding statement explicitly states that it rejects what it considers "tyrannical positive law" (al-kufr bi-al-qawanin al-wad'iyya al-taghutiyya). In June 2013, it announced the formation of its branch in the city of Sirte, along with a founding statement that shares the same ideological spirit as the mother group.[263]

As to its program, the group is unsurprisingly committed to the principle of jihad, "for it is ongoing until the Day of Judgment," as well as to applying God's Law through both preaching the Qur'an and jihad.[264] The group is also keen to proclaim that it is capable of mounting jihad, releasing photographs of a military parade featuring weapons along with banners supporting

---

[261] The FBI is leading the investigation into the killing of Ambassador Stevens, at the time of publishing this report, the investigation is ongoing. For an overview of the suspects in the investigation, see Karen deYoung, "U.S. officials identify extremist groups in the Benghazi attack," *The Washington Post*, 10 September 2013, http://articles.washingtonpost.com/2013-09-10/world/41937113_1_benghazi-attack-accountability-review-board-house-republicans

[262] "Libya: 'Ansar al-Shari'a' tatakhalla 'an al-Silah wa-Tattajihu nahwa al-'Amali al-Da'awiyy," Mufakkiratu al-Islami, 24 October 2012, http://www.islammemo.cc/akhbar/arab/2012/10/14/157185.html (link accessed on the same day).

[263] *Shabakat Shumukh al-Islam*, 28 June 2013, https://shamikh1.info/vb/showthread.php?t=207397&highlight=%E1%ED%C8%ED%C7

[264] "Da'watuna: Nahnu Ansar al-Shari'a," *Shabakat Ansar al-Mujahidin*, 20 January 2013, http://www.as-ansar.com/vb/showthread.php?t=79121 (last accessed 18 May 2013).

Shari'a and rejecting democracy.[265] The pictures are accompanied with a dedication to various jihadi leaders, including Mulla 'Umar, Ayman al-Zawahiri; to leaders of regional jihadi groups; and to the memory of Abu Yahya al-Libi.[266]

Despite displaying its militant capacity and its sympathy with global jihad, the group's preoccupation lies with welfare and law enforcement. It proudly posted a series of photographs about its involvement in a food distribution campaign at the beginning of Ramadan in 2013.[267] On the law enforcement front, it is keen to advertise that it is entrusted with protecting schools where drug traffickers have settled. The group's spokesperson took pride in highlighting that the traffickers were removed without resorting to violence,[268] and to show that the group captured drugs that were being trafficked.[269] Further, a series of photographs were posted on *Shabakat Shumukh al-Islam* depicting patrol units displaying Ansar al-Shari'a's banner that are said to provide security in Benghazi city.[270] It is worth noting that the group displayed its contribution to and solidarity with the Syrian rebels by sending first-aid and other medical support to Syria via Turkey, rather than by sending foreign fighters or weapons.

An illustration of the tension between Ansar al-Shari'a's rhetorical commitment to militancy and its inaction was when it announced that on 2 August 2013 Ahmad 'Ali al-Tir, the leader of its battalion branch in Sirte, was martyred by a battalion that the group claims harbors elements from Qadhafi's supporters. This occurred when Ansar al-Shari'a was carrying out its usual law-enforcement activities; the statement reports that on this occasion it arrested people who were stealing electricity and who were ultimately identified as Qadhafi supporters. This led to

---

[265] The pictures were posted by a correspondent on *Shabakat Shumukh al-Islam*, 10 June 2012, https://shamikh1.info/vb/showthread.php?t=165729&highlight=%E1%ED%C8%ED%C7 (last accessed 9 August 2013).
[266] *Ibid*.
[267] *Shabakat Shumukh al-Islam*, July 2013, https://shamikh1.info/vb/showthread.php?t=205966&highlight=%E1%ED%C8%ED%C7
[268] 15 January 2013, video showing that a school entrusted Ansar al-Shari'a with its security against drug users who were in school. https://www.facebook.com/photo.php?v=135087963319260&set=vb.523934694286554&type=3&permPage=1 (last accessed 18 May 2013).
[269] For video footage depicting narcotics ostensibly seized during anti-trafficking operations, see: https://www.facebook.com/photo.php?v=120237594823093&set=vb.523934694286554&type=3&permPage=1 (last accessed 18 May 2013.
[270] *Shabakat Shumukh al-Islam*, https://shamikh1.info/vb/showthread.php?t=202639&highlight=%E1%ED%C8%ED%C7

clashes between the two battalions, resulting in the death of al-Tir. Yet the statement of the group does not make threats to avenge his death, nor does it use it as an excuse to mount jihadi activities.[271]

Ansar al-Shari'a was again tested in November 2013 when clashes between it and the Libyan army were reported. Ansar al-Shari'a was quick to release a statement intended to explain "to our people in Benghazi what actually happened." The group claimed that they were not responsible for the initiation of the clashes; instead, they responded after they were fired at by a patrol unit that injured some of their men.[272] Perhaps fearing or wishing to avoid further clashes, the group released another statement a week later, asserting that "we have not and will not shed the blood of Muslims even if this were to cost us our stronghold. [We would rather that] the world vanishes and we and our group and projects perish with it than [to live with the burden] of unjustly shedding the blood of a Muslim.[273]

Concluding notes

If global jihadi leaders are struggling to present a coherent ideological framework in response to the Arab Spring, new jihadi groups that emerged in Tunisia, Egypt and Libya are facing a doubly difficult challenge to present a comprehensive program that brings together their rhetoric and their activities. Notwithstanding their vocal presence in the media, new jihadi groups are yet to provide an internally coherent outline of their political identity in general and of their commitment to jihad in particular. That they reject forming political parties and contesting elections is a clear stance that displays their disapproval of positive law. But it is their commitment to pursue all Islamic legal means, including jihad, to implement God's Law that is increasingly highlighting a glaring difference between their rhetoric and their deeds.

How far can they sustain their inaction? Of course they face a catch-22 dilemma: on the one hand they benefit from the fruits of the Arab Spring even though they do not acknowledge this. They enjoy the freedoms, however limited, to promote their worldview in public; and for those

---

[271] *Ibid.*
[272] Ansar al-Shari'a, 25 November 2013, https://twitter.com/AnsarShariaa_ly (accessed 27 November 2013).
[273] Ibid.

who have been invited to broadcast their views in the mainstream media, they appear to enjoy it. On the other hand, they are cognizant that should they translate their rhetoric into action, the security apparatus is unlikely to be forgiving. Indeed, they appear to pride themselves on proving the regimes wrong when violent incidents occur which they are accused of executing but for which they are not responsible.

What then is their political identity? Their inaction removes them from traditional jihadism and their refusal to contest elections places them outside the political process altogether. For now, they retain indeterminate political identity.

CONCLUDING REMARKS

The Arab Spring in Perspective: What about Syria?

The Middle East and North Africa (MENA) region has witnessed regime change in Tunisia, Egypt and Libya since the onset of the Arab Spring. For decades the region has suffered from a democratic deficit to which scholars and analysts have devoted considerable research, with some explanations positing that Arab or Islamic exceptionalism make the region resistant to democratization.[274] It appeared that autocratic regimes were tied to the region's destiny; that is perhaps why the region also has endured a surfeit of jihadis devoted to bringing down dictators through jihad and replacing them with a system of government founded on divine Law.

When people took to the streets carrying banners calling for democracy and the rule of law, cultural theories explaining the democratic deficit had to be revisited. In less than a year, three dictators fell – in Tunisia, Egypt and Libya; Yemen's dictator was forced to resign; and another – the Syrian president – has been fighting for over two years to maintain his hold on power. The ousting of Muhammad Mursi, the elected President of Egypt, and the removal of his government – with the Muslim Brotherhood (MB) in the majority – by the Egyptian military has disrupted the democratic political process in Egypt. Nevertheless, although this has led to an increase in attacks by Gaza-based jihadi groups, it has not caused the MB to renege on its commitment to the democratic process. Countries that underwent regime change confront a long path before they prove themselves as democracies, let alone as consolidated ones. However, notwithstanding the intermittent violence that plague these countries,[275] the Arab

---

[274] See among many, Alfred Stepan with Graeme B. Robertson, "An 'Arab' more than 'Muslim' Electoral Gap," Journal of Democracy, vol. 14, no. 3, July 2003, pp. 30-44; Bernard Lewis, "Why Turkey is the only Muslim Democracy," *The Middle East Quarterly*, March 1994, pp. 41-49. It is also worth reading the article published in the aftermath of the Arab Spring and how should scholars revisit the topic of democratization by Alfred Stepan and Juan J. Linz, "Democratization Theory and the Arab Spring, *Journal of Democracy*, vol. 24, no. 2, April 2013, pp. 15-30.
[275] See introduction to this report about violence and regime change/transition.

Spring has shown that there is at least a rhetorical commitment to democracy by most political actors in the region.

If the democratic deficit theory is to be revisited, what relevance does jihadism have to the region? Many analysts feared that the Arab Spring may at least in the short-term serve as fertile ground in which jihadism would proliferate. Indeed, the emergence of groups projecting a militant worldview in Tunisia, Egypt and Libya in the wake of the Arab Spring may lead the casual observer to surmise that there is a causal link between the two.

But as the previous two chapters have shown, while the success or failure of the Arab Spring remains an open question, jihadism has not fared as well as some feared since the onset of the Arab Spring. Global jihadi leaders have lost key elements that once served as the cornerstone of their ideology's plausibility in the eyes of its adherents. To begin with, like the rest of the world community, the events took them by surprise. Having developed a political identity premised on the deed of jihad, they suddenly found themselves not as instigators, but as spectators of the drama that brought down the dictators. Beyond sincerely rejoicing at the dictators' demise, jihadi leaders were nevertheless confronted by two concerns: (1) the Arab Spring undermined the core premise of their worldview, namely that jihad is the only solution to bringing down dictators; and (2) when people freed from the yoke of dictators decided, by their own free will, that they wanted to pursue the electoral path towards democracy, the jihadis found their worldview to be irreconcilable with the desire of the majority. That is because jihadi ideology, like any religious, monotheist worldview, privileges the elites and marginalizes the masses in political governance. Accordingly, the jihadis' discourse in the wake of the Arab Spring began to replace grievances against dictators with resentment of the people. Ironically and paradoxically, jihadi ideology is suffering from dictator withdrawal symptoms, and jihadi leaders impart the impression of being politically orphaned.

As to the new jihadi groups that emerged in Tunisia, Egypt and Libya, they also suffer from a crisis of identity. Many of them had established their credentials when they took up jihad against the ancien régime of dictators and as a result suffered exile or imprisonment; now they owe their new public existence to the transitioning regimes, the very regimes whose legitimacy they do not recognize. In some ways, they are more like the bastard offspring of autocratic regimes and democratizing ones. The glaring tension in their political identity is their commitment to a jihadi worldview in word and on paper, but not in deed. On the one hand, they proclaim all the trappings of global jihad and do not waste an opportunity to highlight the illegitimacy of their home regimes; on the other hand, they refrain from mounting jihad against the existing political system and spend considerable energy defending themselves against accusations that they intend to do so. The purpose of their militant view is ambiguous at best.

If jihadism has not fared well in the wake of the Arab Spring, the reader of the previous two chapters must surely ask: "what about Syria?" Indeed, a study of the effects of the Arab Spring on jihadism cannot ignore the Syrian militant landscape. The rest of this concluding chapter does not seek to untangle the complexity of the Syrian conflict and its militant landscape. But in view of the conflict's transformation from a peaceful local movement into a violent one, it breaks the pattern that the Arab Spring has followed, even if one were to account for the military intervention in Libya. Further, with the involvement of foreign fighters on the side of the Syrian regime as well as on that of the rebels, the conflict has now become an arena for the contest of political differences between regional and international actors.[276]

For the purpose of this report, the question that must be posed is the following: does the violent conflict in Syria restore credibility in the jihadis' motto that "jihad is the only solution"? More precisely, does Syria restore to the jihadi narrative what Tunisia, Egypt and to some extent Libya have taken away? This concluding chapter argues that the events in Syria could have restored the credibility of jihadism, but that competition between the Islamic State of Iraq (and the Levant) and the Syria-based jihadi group Jabhat al-Nusra (JN) has confused jihadi supporters and earned the derision of their opponents.

---

[276] See Muhammed Ayoob, "The Arab Spring: Its Geostrategic Significance," *Middle East Policy*, Vol. XIX, No. 3, Fall 2012, pp. 84-6.

From *"Silmiyya, Silmiyya"* (Peaceful, Peaceful) to Armed Rebellion

When people took to the streets in Syria in March 2011, their protest followed the peaceful pattern set by Tunisians, Egyptians and initially Libyans. In the early phase the peaceful intent of the Syrian revolution was clearly understood by strategists among jihadis. When Bashar al-Asad's regime accused the rebels of being jihadi terrorists, an authorized joint statement signed by several jihadi websites and media centers – among them *Shabakat Shumukh al-Islam, Shabakat al-Fida' al-Islamiyya* and *Shabakat Ansar al-Mujahidin* – warned against the temptation to resort to violence in Syria. The statement particularly warned those with jihadi leanings, who had been released by the regime – apparently to introduce violence into peaceful protest and sow discord among the opposition – to avoid engaging in militant action lest they give credibility to the regime's false charges. The statement explicitly declares:

> Our brethren should not think that militant activities would be well received by the Syrian people at present so long as the slogan of the people in their revolution is 'peaceful … peaceful' (*silmiyya – silmiyya*). The people will [undoubtedly] reject any group that would adopt militant means in resisting the regime.[277]

At that time, jihadi media were more acutely aware of the peaceful intent of the revolution than the Syrian regime. Mainstream media reports suggest that it was not the protesters, but the regime that was the first to turn to violence against the peaceful protesters, beginning in Der'a,[278] and the predominant face of the armed rebellion against the regime was initially The Free Syrian Army (FSA), which was at pains to project a secular and inclusive image of the military resistance in Syria.

The founding statement of the FSA on 29 March 2012 declares that it will consider "the security forces carrying out the killings of civilians and placing siege on cities as lawful targets and we

---

[277] "Bayan Nusra li-Thawrat Ahlina fi Surya wa-Tanbih li-Khadi'at al-Nizam fi al-Ifraj 'an al-Ikhwa," *Shabakat Ansar al-Mujahidin*, posted 15 July 2011, http://as-ansar.com/vb/showthread.php?t=43703&highlight=%D3%E1%E3%ED%C9 (last accessed 22 May 2013).
[278] Lina Sinjab, "Syria conflict: from peaceful protest to civil war," *BBC*, 15 March 2013, *BBC*, http://www.bbc.co.uk/news/world-middle-east-21797661 (last accessed 2 July 2013).

shall attack them across all Syrian territories." The FSA pledged that it is committed to "establishing a state [governed by] civil [authorities] on the basis of democracy, justice, equality and freedom"; to "applying international humanitarian law, particularly those pertaining to the protection of civilians and civilian targets"; and that it "forbids its members from being part of a political or religious group and from partaking in the political process after bringing down the Asad regime."[279]

Escalation of the conflict led to the proliferation of militant groups in Syria, some of which act under the umbrella of the FSA yet espouse Islamist views and even an anti-democratic agenda. While the FSA claims that it is responsible for most of the attacks against the regime, it is widely believed that armed opposition groups operate independently.[280] Other militant groups acting strictly under the banner of Islam also emerged, the two dominant groups serving as the umbrella organizations for various factions being al-Jabha al-Islamiyya al-Suriyya (Syrian Islamic Front) and Jabhat Tahriri Surya al-Islamiyya (Syria Liberation Front). These are not all clear as to their ideology; such groups have not explicitly rejected a nationalist agenda, as one would expect from hardcore jihadis, and have been prepared to enter into coalitions with other armed groups.[281] The first group to emerge on the Syrian scene with a clear jihadi agenda was Jabhat al-Nusra (JN), and while it mounted joint military operations with other groups, it has not merged with any. To maintain a firm grip on the content of its publicly released materials, the group publishes its statements on the jihadi forums exclusively through its own media arm.

---

[279] The Free Syrian Army, "al-Qiyada al-Mushtaraka li-al-Jaysh al-Suri al-Hurr fi al-Dakhil: Bayan al-Ta'sis," 29 March 2012, CTC Library.
[280] Joshua Landis, "The Syrian Uprising of 2011: Why the Asad Regime is Likely to Survive to 2013," *Middle East Policy*, Vol. XIX, No. 1 (February), 2012.
[281] See for example "Mithaq al-Jabha al-Islamiyya al-Suriyya," *Shabakat Ansar al-Mujahidin*, CTC Library. It should be noted that another charter under a similar name, al-Jabha al-Islamiyya, was released in November 2013. It is not clear whether it is the same coalition of groups. That is because some but not all the signatories on the earlier charter are listed on the recent one. What is important to note is that the group Harakat Ahrar al-Sham al-Islamiyya, which is one of the strongest groups on the Syrian scene was a signatory to the first charter and is now a signatory to the recent charter. See also the various statements released on the website of Jabhat Tahrir Surya al-Islamiyya, http://syrialiberationfront.net.

The Founding of Jabhat al-Nusra

Although JN was officially founded in January 2012, news of its imminent formation was announced in December 2011 when a participant on a jihadi forum wrote that "a new jihadi group has been formed" in Syria, that its members were sent by the Islamic State of Iraq (ISI) and that the group was led by "one of al-Zarqawi's good soldiers." Before long, the group Jabhat al-Nusra li-Ahli al-Sham was using jihadi websites to publicize its presence, releasing an audio-recording by its leader Abu Muhammad al-Julani. While al-Julani did not explicitly indicate the relationship of his group with the ISI, his jihadi leanings were evident: "when calls [inviting the participation of] the people of jihad began to be voiced, we could not but respond to this call and return to our people and our homeland within months of the start of the revolution."[282] He went on to criticize the various opposition factions seeking Western support to oust al-Asad, condemning their endeavor as "a great crime and huge catastrophe that cannot be forgiven."[283]

Over a year since its founding, JN appeared prepared to initiate a program intended to restore credibility in jihadism, at least in the Levant. To begin with, the circumstances in Syria demonstrated that not all dictators are ousted equally; that while some can be ousted through peaceful protest, others cannot. Revolutions against the latter tend to provide fertile ground for violent groups to emerge, an opportunity that JN used to distinguish itself by focusing attention on the deed of jihad and not only its rhetoric. Indeed, with the rise of JN, the jihadis had carved out a steady path for themselves comprising a participatory role in the Arab Spring, which by that time needed to accommodate armed rebellion. If the Arab Spring undermined the jihadi narrative and took active jihad out of jihadism in the countries that underwent regime change, its effects on Syria led to the opening of a militant space that has energized jihadis and provided them overt "employment." Such roles are overt and even welcomed. For example, when in

---

[282] Transcript of the founding statement/speech by Abu Muhammad al-Julani, *Shabakat al-Jihad al-'Alami*, posted on 12 February 2012, http://www.aljahad.com/vb/showthread.php?t=24435
[283] *Ibid.*

December 2012 JN was listed on the United States' Foreign Terrorist Organizations' (FTOs) list, secular Syrian political opposition forces disapproved and complained publicly.[284]

The group also conducted itself in a manner that is by far more disciplined than regional jihadi groups that have arisen after al-Qa'ida ceased to maintain a safe haven in Afghanistan. JN's statements largely focused on the group's operational activities and avoided engaging in heavy ideological discussions. For example, they avoided sectarianism or commitment to global jihad, and the operations they claimed to have carried out targeted the regime's forces and avoided civilian casualties. It is possible that the group opted for less ideology because it was keen to dissociate itself from ISI, whose indiscriminate attacks in Iraq have long worried al-Qa'ida's leadership, as evident in internal communications captured in Bin Ladin's compound in Abbottabad.[285] By contrast, JN has been reported to have been playing an effective role on the operational military front against the Syrian regime,[286] and the group is said to be carrying out attacks against Hizbullah in Lebanon.[287]

In its nascent phase the situation for JN could not have been improved due to its effective conduct on the battlefield, and even its initial dealings with the populace. When asked about JN, Riad al-As'ad, the former Syrian Air Force Colonel and now the Commander of the FSA, praised the group:

> [Members of] JN are our brethren. Thus far, they have proven their capacity to
> fight. Their conduct with people is very agreeable; until now, they have not
> harmed any civilians, on the contrary. It is possible that we may differ with
> them on some ideas. I can tell you that many people are now sympathetic with
> JN. That is because of the various leaderships that have been created by outside
> forces and have created a condition of imbalance internally. We used to have a

---

[284] Al-Tahir Ibrahim, "al-Asbab al-Khafiyya Wara' Wad' Obama 'Jabhat al-Nusra' 'ala Qa'imat al-Irhab," *al-'Asr*, 26 January 2013, http://alasr.ws/articles/view/14001 (last accessed 5 May 2013).

[285] See Nelly Lahoud, Stuart Caudill, Liam Collins, Gabriel Koehler-Derrick, Muhammad al-'Ubaydi and Don Rassler, Letters from Abbottabad: Bin Ladin Sidelined?, *CTC Report*, 3 May 2012, pp. 22-8.

[286] Tim Arango, Anne Barnard and Hwaida Saad, "Syrian Rebels tied to Al Qaeda Play a Key Role in War," *The New York Times*, 8 December 2012, http://www.nytimes.com/2012/12/09/world/middleeast/syrian-rebels-tied-to-al-qaeda-play-key-role-in-war.html?pagewanted=all (last accessed 2 July 2013).

[287] *Shabakat Shumukh al-Islam*, posted 20 February 2013.

single leader by the name Bashar al-Asad, now we have many. JN is a sincere

group that is not driven by any external loyalties.[288]

It is not surprising that al-Zawahiri had praise of his own, although he did not specifically

address JN in his statements, and instead used the more general and inclusive designation of

"Usud al-Sham" (the lions of the Levant). Al-Zawahiri had been encouraging Syrians who rose

up against the regime before the formation of JN; in July 2011, he released a statement entitled

"'Izzu al-Sharqi Awwaluhu Dimashq," which roughly translates into "Damascus is the

beginning [of the march towards reclaiming] the dignity of the East."[289] In it he appealed to the

Syrians not to be fooled by U.S. support of their cause: "I assume that you will not be deceived

by the ruses of the imperial global powers and the new Crusader tricks," he said, and went on

to add that "America that had accommodated Bashar al-Asad throughout his reign today

pretends to be standing by your side only because it saw the seismic extent of your anger."[290]

Around the time when JN was officially formed, al-Zawahiri released a statement, entitled "Ila

al-Amami Ya Usud al-Sham" (Lions of the Levant March Forward) in which he was more

explicit about calling for jihad in Syria.[291] But within months of the formation of JN, and no

doubt having been informed of its battlefield success, al-Zawahiri was hopeful regarding jihadis

in Syria. In a statement calling for unity around the concept of *tawhid*, he conducts a *tour

d'horizon* of various Islamic regions, applauding the heroism of Muslims at the same time as

displaying concern for their lack of unity; nonetheless, his section on Syria has an optimistic

tone. It is so optimistic that, despite admitting his limitations in composing poetry, he could not

halt the urge to compose a poem that "I hope that the lions of Islam in the Levant and Iraq will

accept [as a token of my respect]."[292]

---

[288] Riyad al-As'ad (interview), posted 19 March 2013,
https://www.youtube.com/watch?v=RWrZhQG4leg&feature=player_embedded (last accessed 4 July 2013).
[289] Ayman al-Zawahiri, "'Izzu al-Sharqi Awwaluhu Dimashq," *Shabakat Ansar al-Mujahidin*, 28 July2011, http://as-ansar.com/vb/showthread.php?t=44649&highlight=%C3%E6%E1%E5.
[290] *Ibid*.
[291] Ayman al-Zawahiri, "Ila al-Amam Ya Usud al-Sham," January 2012, CTC Library.
[292] Ayman al-Zawahiri, "Tawhid al-Kalima hawla Kalimat al-Tawhid," *Shabakat al-Fida' al-Islamiyya*, April 2013, CTC Library.

What's in a Name?

For over a year it appeared that as long as the violent conflict continued in Syria, JN would make gains through its disciplined military operations. Even though for an extended period the group did not commit itself explicitly to global jihad, its actions were nevertheless bound to reflect well on global jihad. This changed when the ISI took a unilateral decision to merge with their brethren in JN, a merger that al-Julani only learned of subsequently through the media.[293]

What caused ISI to surprise JN with an imposed merger? Was ISI resentful that JN's mainstream popularity was eclipsing its own? Or was it concerned that the popularity JN was enjoying among the populace in Syria might lead the group to form a political party and contest elections if Bashar's regime should fall? Regardless of ISI's rationale, the statement released by its leader Abu Bakr al-Husayni al-Qurashi al-Baghdadi, announcing the "glad tidings" of the merger, had an unmistakably haughty tone to it that must have infuriated al-Julani. He pitched the merger of his group with JN as a form of elevating JN to a higher rank. Al-Baghdadi explained that it is "permissible to cancel the names of jihadi groups and replace them with ones commensurate with their [higher level of] development and nobility ... new names that would make us forget the previous ones despite our affection for them."[294]

Al-Baghdadi proceeded to illustrate this with the example of Iraq, which saw Abu Mus'ab al-Zarqawi launch his jihad first under the name of "al-Tawhid wa-al-Jihad," before his group's name changed to "Qa'idat al-Jihad in Mesopotamia."[295] This occurred, according to al-Baghdadi, when the group acquired "a more noble position and higher rank after al-Zarqawi pledged allegiance to Sheikh Usama Bin Ladin, the leader of al-Qa'ida."[296] It is not clear how al-Baghdadi could rationalize, from a religious perspective, that replacing a name grounded in the

---

[293] Abu Muhammad al-Julani, "Hawla Sahat al-Sham," *Shabakat al-Fida' al-Islamiyya*, April 2013, http://alfidaa.org/vb/showthread.php?t=60881

[294] Abu Bakr al-Husayni al-Qurashi al-Baghdadi, "Wa-Bashshir al-Mu'minin," *Shabakat Shumukh al-Islam*, April 2013, CTC Library.

[295] It should be noted that when al-Zarqawi's pledge of allegiance was accepted by Bin Ladin, the name of his group changed to al-Qa'ida in Mesopotamia and not "Qa'idat al-Jihad in Mesopotamia." Nelly Lahoud remarked that the name "Qa'idat al-Jihad" was not used by Bin Ladin in his public statements. See her "The Merger of al-Shabab and Qa'idat al-Jihad," *CTC Sentinel*, 16 February 2012, footnote 6.

[296] *Ibid.*

theological premise of *tawhid* with a non-religious name like "al-Qa'ida" would "please God," as he asserted.[297]

If al-Baghdadi's knowledge of Islamic religious principles could benefit from improvement, his ability to formulate neutral and inoffensive political statements is also entirely lacking. His "glad tidings" unwittingly demote al-Qa'ida under the leadership of Bin Ladin, explaining that al-Zarqawi's group again changed its name to "Majlis Shura al-Mujahidin" when "the souls of its members grew higher in ranks as they were elevated through jihad," seemingly progressing ahead of Bin Ladin and his group. Then jihad in Iraq, al-Baghdadi continues, reached an even more "blessed" rank with the declaration of the new name the "Islamic State of Iraq" (ISI) under the leaderships of Abu 'Umar al-Baghdadi and Abu Hamza al-Misri. Al-Baghdadi proudly remarks that through declaring ISI these leaders were effectively "charting a path for us that does not recognize borders, and formulating an [ideological] program that does not discriminate between nations and races." It is as if a borderless *umma* and equality among races and nations on the basis of common belief in the Islamic creed had not previously been formulated by other jihadi leaders or ideologues. Since ISI obtained an elevated rank, al-Baghdadi decided that their brethren in the Levant were lagging behind and needed help so that they too might rise in rank. They "had established cells limited to training" for jihad, that is why, he continues, ISI decided to support them:

> We commissioned al-Julani, who is one of our soldiers, along with a group the
> members of which are ours, and we sent them from Iraq to the Levant so that
> they may join our cells there. We prepared a work plan and a way forward for
> them, and we supported them financially and on a monthly basis with half of
> what is in the treasury. We also sent them men, *muhajirun* and *ansar* [i.e.,
> Syrians and foreign fighters], who are experienced in battle … thus the
> authority of the ISI extended to the Levant but we did not make it public for
> security reasons so that people may see for themselves the truth of this State
> away from the distortion and falsehood of the media. It is now time that we

---

[297] al-Baghdadi, "Wa-Bashshir al-Mu'minin."

declare to the people of the Levant and the entire world that JN is but an extension of ISI and part of it … that is why we now declare that the names "ISI" and "JN" are henceforth cancelled, and we combine them under a single name "The Islamic State in Iraq and the Levant (ISIL)."

Why had the time come to merge the two groups? Al-Julani's response two days later to al-Baghdadi suggests that he does not have the answer to this question. He sought vainly to compose a diplomatic response, prefacing it with "if the statement attributed to [Abu Bakr al-Baghdadi] is true, [it should be known] that we were not consulted."[298] He highlighted the gratitude he and members of his group owe to the "great generosity" they received from their brethren in Iraq. On a more sensitive note, he acknowledged that while he had met with al-Baghdadi, it was he who proposed a plan to support the people of the Levant and to which al-Baghdadi agreed. He explained that their agreement was "to re-establish God's authority," but they did not discuss the issue of declaring a state. As far as an "Islamic State in the Levant," al-Julani asserted, this would be established through all those who supported it and when the local circumstances allowed it.

Not only did al-Julani reject the merger with ISI: he went on to cut al-Baghdadi down to size. He concluded his response by accepting al-Baghdadi's call that it is incumbent upon jihadis to pursue a higher, nobler rank, and that is why "I pledge, on behalf of members of JN and their leader, to renew our allegiance to the Sheikh of jihad, Sheikh Ayman al-Zawahiri, may God protect him."[299]

What's in a name? More precisely, which name will Ayman al-Zawahiri use?

A letter attributed to al-Zawahiri and addressed to both al-Baghdadi and al-Julani was released by al-Jazeera in June 2013.[300] At the same time as praising both groups and lauding their

---

[298] Abu Muhammad al-Julani, "Hawla Sahat al-Sham," *Shabakat al-Fida' al-Islamiyya*, April 2013, http://alfidaa.org/vb/showthread.php?t=60881 (last accessed 4 July 2013).
[299] *Ibid*.
[300] "Al-Zawahiri Yulghi Damj 'Jihadiyyi' Suriya wa-al-'Iraq," *al-Jazeera*, 9 June 2013, http://www.aljazeera.net/news/pages/a5a7d33e-3c9f-4706-b070-e358b5e67236 (last accessed 4 July 2013). The leaked letter may be accessed on the same link.

respective sacrifices – a form of diplomacy – al-Zawahiri also chastised the leaders of both for making public announcements without consulting him. He places blame on both leaders and proceeds to annul "The Islamic State in Iraq and the Levant." Perhaps anticipating further disputes between the two groups, al-Zawahiri appoints a certain Abu Khaled al-Suri, "our representative in the Levant," as an arbiter who would set up a legal court to settle differences between the two groups. The identity of Abu Khaled is not known, but given that al-Zawahiri describes him as someone "among the finest we have known," he appears to hold a senior status and likely to have training in Islamic law.

The letter's authenticity was initially debated, yet the official spokesman for ISI Abu Muhammad al-'Adnani al-Shami responded to the letter and denounced its content regardless, even though he acknowledged that it is "attributed" to al-Zawahiri.[301] The letter, he complained, seeks to "divide one of the largest jihadi groups" into a Syrian group and an Iraqi one, as if it is conforming to the borders demarcated by the Sykes-Picot, in reference to the agreement between Britain and France, which divided the Middle East between themselves in anticipation of the fall of the Ottoman empire. Al-'Adnani went on to question the rationale behind ordering the withdrawal of the ISI and its jihadis from the Levant so that each group would fight in its own territory. Yet nowhere does the letter attributed to al-Zawahiri give such orders. Instead, the letter calls on each group to support the other in so far as it is possible, be it through sending men, money or weapons. It is either that al-'Adnani did not carefully read the letter, or he was referring to another more extensive letter that al-Zawahiri or perhaps Abu Khaled al-Suri may have sent.

On 8 November 2013, an audio-recording of the same letter by al-Zawahiri was released by al-Jazeera, thus confirming its veracity. Members on jihadi forums were quick to show their disappointment, one member accused Abu Khaled of leaking the letter and held him responsible; another declared that since "al-Baghdadi did not pledge allegiance to al-Zawahiri or al-Qa'ida, and therefore the Islamic State [of Iraq and the Levant] has nothing to do with

---

[301] Abu Muhammad al-'Adnani, *al-Minbar al-I'lami al-Jihadi*, 20 June 2013, http://alplatformmedia.com/vb/showthread.php?t=24303 (accessed 25 June 2013).

them, in fact it is al-Qa'ida which pledged allegiance to the ISIL, not the reverse."[302] The messages were swiftly deleted. It is not clear whether the audio-recording was leaked to al-Jazeera or whether it was sent with the full knowledge of al-Zawahiri because he no longer trusts jihadi websites. This represents a new era for jihadism. If the divides among jihadis in the post-9/11 era was kept a relatively private affair under the leadership of Bin Ladin – as the released Abbottabad documents suggest – the leadership of al-Zawahiri is marked by public divisions.

Al-Zawahiri's dilemma is unenviable; he should perhaps take a page from Bin Ladin's book and use generic designations such as "jihadis" instead of embracing regional jihadi groups that pledge allegiance to him and later prove to be a liability rather than an asset to global jihad. It is possible that al-Zawahiri is acceding to posthumous lessons from Bin Ladin. His September 2013 statement under the heading "General Guidelines for Jihadi Work" is likely inspired by Bin Ladin's memorandum of understanding that he had tasked 'Atiyya to draft before he died. Bin Ladin had been concerned as to the indiscriminate attacks carried out by jihadis and had wanted regional jihadi leaders to agree to conform to a code of conduct in their activities.[303] Al-Zawahiri, who was unrestrained in bestowing the "al-Qa'ida" brand upon regional jihadi groups, perhaps against the wishes of Bin Ladin, may now be reconsidering his previous enthusiasm.[304] His recent *Guidelines* seeks to police, in his own diplomatic ways, the activities of regional jihadi groups, imploring them to avoid targeting non-combatants, including non-Muslims.[305]

To return to the question posed earlier: does Syria restore to the jihadi narrative what Tunisia, Egypt and to some extent Libya has taken away? On the one hand, the conflict has certainly broken the pattern of political change that the Arab Spring had followed and has introduced jihad to its theater. The militant landscape in Syria has been serving as a magnet for foreign

---

[302] These postings were quickly printed before they were deleted by the websites.
[303] Letters from Abbottabad, pp. 14-19.
[304] *Ibid*, p. 55. See also Nelly Lahoud, "The Merger of Al-Shabab and Qa`idat al-Jihad," *CTC Sentinel* 5, no. 2 (2012).
[305] Ayman al-Zawahiri, "Tawjihatun 'Ammatun li-al-'Amali al-Jihadi," 14 September 2013, https://shamikh1.info/vb/showthread.php?t=211363 (last accessed 2 August 2013).

fighters from different parts of the Muslim world. It is not just enthusiast young fighters from, among other countries, Chechnya and the Caucasus regions, but also, as the footage from one remarkable You Tube clip shows, an entire family of three generations emigrating from Kazakhstan to Syria. It shows female and male children reciting the Qur'an (*tajwid*) and young men speaking about the virtues of jihad to explain their long journey.[306] But the inclusion of jihad in the Syrian conflict has mixed resonance in regard to the development of the Arab Spring. In some ways the violent Syrian conflict has provided an arena in which enthusiast Tunisian, Egyptian and Libyan jihadis can vent their jihad instead of destabilizing their home countries. One You Tube clip shows a Tunisian jihadi calling on his brethren in Tunisia to cease "preaching the virtues of jihad" (*al-da'wa ila al-jihad*) and join him in "real/active jihad" (*al-jihad al-fi'li*).[307] In this footage he describes the intimate bond he has formed with other jihadis and pities his brethren in Tunisia for not translating their *da'wa* into reality, warning them that they will need to answer to God on the Day of Judgment.[308] From the Tunisian government's perspective, Tunisia's security is safer with such a jihadi abroad.

Further, while Syria had the potential to enable jihad to be part of the future of the Arab Spring, the ISI averted this. As it stands, and although attempts at rapprochement between JN and ISI are promoted frequently,[309] groups operating under the banner of Islam in Syria are choosing sides – and in some instances this has caused schisms within the same group; insisting on their independence; or rejecting both groups altogether. For example, the Syria Liberation Front wasted no time criticizing the declaration of the Islamic State of Iraq and the Levant, rejecting it as outsiders imposing their will on Syrians.[310] The group did not spare Jabhat al-Nusra either; a You Tube video shows a discussion among members of the group denouncing al-Julani as someone who refuses to reveal anything about himself, questioning those who would pledge

---

[306] See "al-Dawlatu al-Islamiyyatu fi Diyafati 'A'ilatin Muhajira," https://archive.org/details/rasil-10 (last accessed 25 October 2013).

[307] See https://www.youtube.com/watch?v=bBu50KW0PB8&feature=youtu.be (last accessed 25 October 2013).

[308] *Ibid.*

[309] See for example interview with Sami al-'Aridi (from JN), "Manhajuna wa-'Aqidatuna," YouTube, http://www.youtube.com/watch?v=IVxfkleQT5E&feature=youtu.be (last accessed 25 October 2013).

[310] See their official response on their website, http://syrialiberationfront.net/category/%d8%a7%d9%84%d8%a8%d9%8a%d8%a7%d9%86%d8%a7%d8%aa/page /34/ (last accessed 25 October 2013).

allegiance to such a mysterious figure and fight under such a "blind banner."[311] Another more compelling example is that of the foreign militant group, Katibatu al-Muhajirin (The émigrés Brigade),[312] led by Abu 'Umar al-Shishani. The latter seems to have pledged allegiance to al-Baghadadi, limited to the military domain (*bay'at qital*); this was adamantly opposed by another leader in the group, a certain Sayfullah, who, along with sixty members, has since departed from the group.[313]

The potential of the rift between ISIL and JN may have severe repercussions on the course of global jihad. In October, a member on one of the jihadi websites promised a forthcoming "glad tiding" and the intimation that a "major pledge of allegiance" (*bay'a dakhma*) by a group from outside Iraq and the Levant to al-Baghdadi is about to be made public.[314] In December, the same member posted that "some units from amongst the largest groups [in Syria] such as Ahrar al-Sham, Liwa' al-Tawhid, Sham al-Islam, JN, [as well as other units] from Ansar al-Islam (in Iraq) pledged allegiance to ISIL."[315] If this is true, it suggests that ISIL is either actively seeking to divide militant groups operating in Syria or that members among these groups are aligning with the ISIL. More importantly, this suggests that ISIL is not just in competition with JN, but may also be in competition with Qa'idat al-Jihad. The fact that the name ISIL is still in use despite it being annulled by al-Zawahiri in his letter – which has now been authenticated by an audio-recording – suggests that ISIL is willing to be publicly disruptive to the image of global jihad. The implications for al-Zawahiri's symbolic leadership are likely to be tumultuous. A video has been released asserting that ISIL is an organization independent of al-Qa'ida and calling on al-Zawahiri and Mullah 'Umar to pledge allegiance to al-Baghdadi;[316] while the identity of the side that released it is anonymous, the video was posted by a member on a jihadi

---

[311] YouTube, https://www.youtube.com/watch?v=LuzIQARgChU&feature=youtube_gdata_player (last accessed 25 October 2013).

[312] The name was later changed to Jaysh al-Muhajirin wa-al-Ansar.

[313] "Hawla Majmu 'at Sayfullah al-Quqaziyya," https://www.youtube.com/watch?v=yU6K1mq38jw&feature=youtu.be (last accessed 25 October 2013).

[314] "Ajil: Anba' 'an Tamaddud al-Dawla al-Islamiyya," *Shabakat al-Fida' al-Islamiyya*, http://alfidaa.org/vb/showthread.php?t=77616&highlight=%CE%c7%D1%CC (last accessed 25 October 2013).

[315] "Allahu Akbar Bushra Tayyiba," Shabakat al-Fida' al-Islamiyya, 12 December 2013, http://alfidaa.org/vb/showthread.php?t=85509 (accessed on the same day).

[316] YouTube, http://www.youtube.com/watch?v=VgIThfOryP8 (accessed 12 November 2013).

forum for discussion but was later removed.[317] It has been argued that jihadis are more prone to ideological divisions than to unification,[318] but it seems that their attempts at unification are even more divisive than their divisions. Thus, even though the climate of the Arab Spring is experiencing fluctuation in its temperature, for now the jihadis are not in a position to control it.

But it should be recognized that the impact of the events in Syria cannot be objectively assessed until a decisive change takes place in Syria, either in favor or against the regime. If the regime falls, militant groups are bound to undergo either a process of elimination or mergers between them, or a combination of both. Unless jihadi groups are not merely stronger than existing rebel groups combined, but are also united – which is not the case currently and is unlikely to be so during peacetime – then political parties may eventually be formed and elections held. If, however, Bashar's regime maintains its grip on power and regains what the rebels have captured, then this may prove not only that dictators cannot be ousted equally but also that jihad is not the solution.

---

[317] The video was posted by a certain Abu Hamza al-Ansari on 12 November 2013 on *Shabakat Shumukh al-Islam*, https://shamikh1.info/vb/showthread.php?t=214280 (accessed on the same date, the posting has been removed).
[318] Nelly Lahoud, The Jihadis' Path to Self-Destruction, New York: Columbia University Press, 2010; Stuart Caudill, Brotherhood or False Rhetoric? Examining Cooperation between al-Qa'ida in the Arabian Peninsula and al-Shabaab, Senior thesis in the Department of Social Sciences, May 2013.